W9-BXE-853

STYLE
TRADITIONS

STYLE
TRADITIONS

Recreating Period Interiors

STEPHEN CALLOWAY AND STEPHEN JONES

RIZZOLI
NEW YORK

To Barry Bucknell, without whom this book would never have been published.

First published in the United States of America in 1990 by
Rizzoli International Publications, Inc., 300 Park Avenue South, New York 10010.

© (Text) Stephen Calloway, 1990.
© The Hamlyn Publishing Group Ltd. 1990.

All rights reserved
No part of this publication may be reproduced, in any manner whatsoever without
permission in writing from Rizzoli International Publications, Inc.

Library of Congress Cataloguing-in-Publication Data
Calloway, Stephen
Traditional Style,
Style traditions: recreating period interiors/Stephen Calloway.
p. cm.
Originally published under title: Traditional style.
Includes index.
ISBN 0-8478-1131-X
1. Interior decoration – Themes, motives. I. Title.
NK2110,C18 1990
747.22 – dc20

Typesetting by Ampersand Typsetting Ltd, Bournemouth, England.
Printed in Great Britain by William Collins Sons & Co Ltd

Senior Commissioning Editor: Judith More
Deputy Art Director: Bobbie Colgate-Stone
Project Manager: John Wainwright
Designed by: The Image
Editor: Sarah Chapman
Picture Researcher: Carol Varley
Directory: Julia Bigham

First published in Great Britain in 1990 by Pyramid Books,
an imprint of the Octopus Publishing Group,
Michelin House, 91, Fulham Road, London SW3 6RB.

CONTENTS

INTRODUCTION

People build houses for many practical and impractical reasons: for shelter and safety; for comfort and delight; for show. However, throughout history the decoration of houses has been guided by motives which, though not always strictly practical, seem to fulfil a universal need to personalize and adorn the spaces in which we live. Thus today decoration has become the one art universally practised; a means of expression both for the harassed professional and the happy amateur.

One of the more difficult distinctions to draw in studying the history of houses is that between simple building and the more considered activity of designing Architecture. At which point does the terraced house cease to be a commercial response to a general need for accommodation and gain the distinction of belonging to an architectural tradition? We all know that the Nash terraces of London's Regent's Park district are Architecture, at least on the outside, but British towns and cities are full of many handsome terraces of the eighteenth and nineteenth centuries which share the pleasing proportions and logical ground-plans of these grander cousins. Such terraces are not generally dignified by the name of

'The Studio' by Leonard Wyburd (1886). This quintessential artist's studio displays the Victorian passion for collecting historically interesting objects at its most evocative. Works of art, armour, ceramics and old musical instruments, all classic artists' 'props', are thrown together with theatrical effect. The recreation today of any traditional style must have something of this stage-set quality. Drama as much as accuracy will set the scene.

*A Bedchamber of about 1690. An unknown painter here reminds us that even the most
magnificent Baroque apartments were the settings for ordinary life. Rich hangings
and trimmings made beds the most important furnishings in any house, and
throughout the lavish use of textiles is the key to the period. Tapestries made a room both
magnificent and snug.*

Architecture, although they enjoy today a renewed respect as more people realise their fundamental virtues. However, the grandest palaces and the simplest of homes have always shared this characteristic: that their owners have, by enriching their rooms, enhanced their lives.

Since the Second World War, and especially in the last ten years, the general awareness and appreciation of interiors has increased vastly, partly as a result of the many grand houses open to the public and equally importantly through the pages of books and glossy magazines. Inevitably, people are therefore more than ever aware of both the shortcomings and the potential of their own homes. Clearly those

few who live surrounded by fine architecture and real period decoration have no need to study their effects. This book is written for owners of more ordinary homes with the desire and boldness to realise their dreams.

Any attempt to recreate the styles of the past must inevitably be as much a matter of theatrical evocation as of scholarly reconstruction. In the final analysis, even the museum curator's painstaking researches and scrupulous methods are allied to an imaginative leap back into history, for it is very seldom the case that every element of an old room survives or is recorded. We continually re-invent the past. In a sense, therefore, the suggestions offered here are

'Interiors', colour plates from Humphrey Repton's **Fragments** *(1816). Repton intended in these contrasting images to show how the austere formality and lack of comfort of the cedar-panelled parlour of 1730 (left) had been superseded by the convenient domestic arrangements of the Regency period (right). Fitted carpetting, upholstered furniture informally grouped and pretty draperies soften the classical architecture and provide an elegant setting for such civilised pursuits as drawing, music making and reading, whereas the parlour of 1730 relies upon good proportions and a plain but handsome chimney-piece for its effect. Sparseness is all and throws into high relief the quality of the furniture.*

historical fiction, but, like so many good stories, they are founded on fact.

On this premise we have divided the history of British decoration into chronological sections describing the characteristic styles of each era. In order to explain the evolution of taste through the four centuries that divide the reign of the first Elizabeth and that of the present Queen of England, each begins with a brief sketch of the social and cultural movements which shaped the decoration of the age. Every style begins as a minority interest cultivated by an intellectual, artistic or aristocratic elite. The ideas of these leaders of taste are rapidly taken up by lively and informed followers of fashion, and

no less speedily disseminated by manufacturers of furnishings.

In the eighteenth century these manufacturers began to publish their designs, so making them available in books or as prints to a vastly increased and more prosperous middle-class audience. In the latter part of this book, therefore, the names of many of the well-known designers – such as Chippendale and Robert Adam – begin to appear as the authors of the style-manuals of their day. Some of these rare books have in recent years been reprinted in paperback, and it is therefore possible to keep them by you when planning a scheme.

Each chapter analyses the elements of decoration

Above: 'Queen Charlotte at her dressing-table' by Johann Zoffany (c.1768). The magnificent setting of this portrait of the wife and sons of George III provides valuable clues as to mid-eighteenth-century taste in furnishings. Notice in particular the green silk festoon curtains, the lace and ribboned draperies of the table and the rich oriental carpet laid on bare boards.

Right: 'An interior' by Sir John Lavery (1926). In this twenties conversation piece, Lady Juliet Duff stands surrounded by French furniture, oriental ceramics and renaissance bronzes. All this opulence reflects a taste favoured by both old and new money from the 1890s up until 1945.

that belong to the period, examining all the pieces of the jig-saw: windows, doors and chimney-pieces; wooden and plaster mouldings on walls and ceilings; paints, papers and textiles; and the furniture and other moveable objects unique to the age. The colours and the ways in which things are arranged tell us as much about historic taste as the permanent elements. Hard as it is to pin down exact colours, we have tried to suggest both particular shades and, more importantly, characteristic combinations. In the same way, we have endeavoured to show the kinds of arrangements which people made of their possessions. Since so much of the history of decoration is deeply personal, and since there are as many

'The Tiled Kitchen' by Harry Bush (1925). Strictly speaking this is the business-end of a kitchen, the scullery. Most houses built before 1930 had a larger, square room, the kitchen proper with the scullery, a tiled area plumbed for water and gas, adjacent; a third distinct space, the larder, was set aside for the storage of food. Here we see a scullery with larder beyond. The tiling, extending half way up the walls, is trimmed with moulded and coloured edging tiles which can still be found today. The free-standing gas cooker had by this date largely supplemented if not replaced the built-in coal-burning range, but gas-lighting was not replaced by electricity in the domestic quarters of many houses until the late 1940s.

'Conversation-piece at The Daye House' by Rex Whistler (1937). Whistler, a friend of Edith Olivier, seen here on her day-bed entertaining a group of literary friends, records a room furnished between the wars in a timeless and elegantly practical taste. Capacious fitted bookcases complement the eighteenth-century panelling, while a happy clutter of old and new furniture is scattered with evidences of literary and rural pursuits. This is the classic English style.

variations on the themes we have described as there are colourful individuals in this story, many sections also include examples of exotic and fantastic experiments made over the years.

There is a time and a place to be deadly serious about tassels and fringes. Throughout this book we have tried to offer the reader an accurate and accessible survey which avoids the pedantry of an academic essay or the well-intentioned but useless generalizations of the average D.I.Y. manual. Always bear in mind that decoration at its best is a game. Play it with panache, aim for grand theatrical statements, and always avoid what Osbert Lancaster so wisely called "the fatal will-o'-the-wisp of period accuracy".

TUDOR

1485 · 1603

AN INTEREST IN INTERIOR decoration implies not only pride of possession but also the leisure to indulge in domestic preoccupations. Domesticity as an indulgence may seem paradoxical to us today, but to ordinary people living under the rule of the first Tudor monarch, Henry VII, the arts of peace and the joys of prosperity were an exciting novelty. Britain's transition from a warring medieval realm to a modern political state began with the conclusion of the Wars of the Roses in 1485. Similarly, domestic life as we understand it today, with its connotations of privacy and ease, emerged as the Englishman's castle gradually became a retreat for the cultivation of life's pleasures rather than protection merely from its dangers.

During this period fashionable taste in decoration was exclusively the preserve of the Court and the great power-brokers of the land. Such patrons saw decoration and the ordering of rooms not only as an aesthetic statement, but as a tangible and indeed essential expression of status. In visual terms, high fashion was manifested increasingly by the use of Renaissance motifs, though these were at first merely grafted onto fundamentally medieval forms.

The Bedroom, Flemyngs Hall, Suffolk. This highly successful and theatrical evocation of Elizabethan decoration bears the hallmark of its creator, Angus McBean, celebrated surrealist photographer and self-confessed 'bodger of genius'. The massive four-poster bed is a confection of some pieces of original carving applied to old timbers and cleverly draped. Much of the effect of the room derives from the rich colouring of the boldly stencilled wall hangings of hessian.

Only as sophistication in architecture and decoration increased towards the end of the sixteenth century, did true classically inspired ideals coming in from the Continent impinge to any significant extent on traditional English domestic architecture. Thus, ordinary middle-class homes, the houses of yeomen and merchants, remained throughout the century essentially medieval in their structure, organization and decoration. Built in stone or on a timber frame, such houses continued to have the simplest of plans in which everything centred on the main room with its massive chimney-piece. By this date, the private solar- and bed-chambers, which had previously only been found in the grandest houses, were becoming more common.

If you are lucky enough to own a sixteenth-century house, it is worth taking infinite pains to ensure that everything you do to it contributes to an authentic effect, and that the materials used are sympathetic to the original structure. On the other hand, the virtues of Elizabethan houses rest so much upon the integrity of the original structure and the beauty of old materials, that an attempt to fabricate from scratch a room of the period in anything but the most theatrical of styles is almost bound to fail.

Given an original structure, certain basic rules apply. The dark staining or, worse, the painting of exposed beams is a solecism dating from no earlier than the nineteenth century, as misleading as that era's predilection for 'olde oake'. The best modern practice is, if necessary, to strip but certainly not to bleach the original timbers and to limit any 'finishing' to the application of suitable preservatives. Doors and window frames in oak or elm may well be original, in which case they should be treated in a similar manner and perhaps given a light wax-polished finish. Most other wooden fittings such as skirting boards are likely to be of a later date and constructed in softwoods that were always intended to be painted.

If doors or window frames are missing, there is really no alternative to employing a skilled joiner to make replacements. The only commercially available door which could possibly work in this context is the type constructed from vertical planks braced by diagonals and more usually retailed as shed doors. All mass-produced doors, studded with bogus iron-mongery or enlivened by an aperture glazed with 'bottle-glass', are anathema. Black-finished iron fittings for doors and windows are in fact appropriate, but seek out those made by small, independent forges in preference to factory-made examples, which all too often come tortured into barley-twist and other over-elaborate forms.

Not every sixteenth-century living room had the capacious inglenook beloved of Hollywood, and the period in fact saw the gradual replacement of the open hearth with the enclosed fireplace framed by a chimney surround. All forms of hearth of the time were equipped with a cast-iron fireback. A pair of fire-dogs (andirons) supported the burning logs, although towards the latter part of the century simple fire-baskets came into use in the cities to enable coal to be burned. In many rooms the open hearth was updated in the seventeenth or eighteenth century with a more convenient chimney-piece and grate. This is in a sense a part of the history of the building, and the decision to remove them will almost

'Sir Nicholas Unton' by an unknown artist, c.1596. In this memorial portrait the subject is surrounded by scenes from his life. Top left is a characteristically sparsely furnished bed-chamber. The four-poster decked with plumes indicates status, though the absence of carpeting other than rush-matting shows how spartan even a courtier's house could be. Display was an important part of Elizabethan decoration. In the dining room pewter and other vessels deck a lavish sideboard, but diners sit on simple cushioned stools.

Left: The panelled parlour, Chastleton House, Oxfordshire. The elaborate plaster ceiling and grand carved chimneypiece are typical of Elizabethan display. Easier to simulate are the historic portraits above the panelling. The furniture is of many dates. The table-cloth is modern, but effective. Above: The library, Sissinghurst Castle, Kent. This room, created in the 1930s by writers Vita Sackville-West and Harold Nicholson, is faked-up within a real Elizabethan shell. Rustic plank bookshelves and a plain plank door echo original timbering.

invariably be too purist, and fail to take into account the accretive nature of period houses.

In houses not grand enough to have panelling, walls were always of bare plaster, limewashed and therefore either white or tinted with earth colours, applied as flatly as possible. Simple freely painted or stencilled decorative schemes do survive as models which can be followed. These were bold, broad and vivacious in execution and most modern stencils fail to capture such qualities. If you wish to add borders,

for example, then look hard at the originals and cut your own stencils or, better still, try to emulate the characteristic motifs and brushstrokes freehand.

Such austerity of effect was relieved and comfort provided by the use of wall hangings. The grandest were of tapestry, but many were of needlework or rich fabrics. Then as now, a cheaper alternative was 'poor man's tapestry' painted on cloth. Large pieces of antique textiles will look well as decorative hangings suspended from simple wooden or metal rods held

up by brackets on the wall. Carpets at this date were rare and laid on the floor only in great palaces. Elsewhere, carpets were used as a richly decorative covering for tables, a striking effect worth reviving today. Floors were scattered with rushes, sweetened with herbs or dried flowers such as lavender. Woven rush matting is the workable substitute today, although many will prefer the historically inaccurate but visually appealing effect of polished bare boards.

Since entirely genuine Elizabethan furniture is extremely rare and expensive, the sparseness characteristic of the age is all too easily achieved. Reproductions of Tudor furniture rarely capture anything but the basic lines of the originals, but will at least allow a complete room-setting to be assembled. Choose only authentic furniture types such as the classic 'blanket-box' with a hinged lid. Several types of cupboard modelled on sixteenth-century prototypes were made in the nineteenth century, and are generally referred to as 'hutch' or 'coal' cupboards. Modern examples can also be found, but avoid those with too much carving, and of course avoid all twentieth-century furniture types such as tea-trolleys or video cabinets masquerading in half-timbering. The same is true of other artefacts, but paintings of the period remind us that the Elizabethan home was uncluttered by useless ornamental objects. Fortunately the kinds of domestic objects which can still be found, pewter plates and dishes and some pieces of ceramic, look well placed singly on polished wood surfaces.

For a century in which the rooms of rich and poor alike were lit by candles and rush-lights, there can be no authentic modern equivalent. Two options only present themselves: the first and more traditional solution has, since the 1920s, been the use of wrought-iron standard lamps and electrified candle-sticks fitted with plain parchment shades. More recently, museum display practice has popularized frankly contemporary, minimalist light fittings, frequently uplighters, which, by their very modernity, efface themselves from competition with the historical elements of the room.

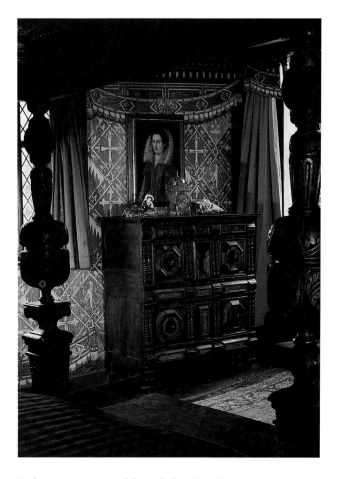

Left: An amusing 'olde-oak' kitchen. Decorator and painter Althea Wilson created this clever play on the Elizabethan style in her London house. Modern kitchen fitments and equipment are dressed-up with stained wood and the walls enlivened with boldly painted motifs and a collection of bogus majolica plates.
Above: Angus McBean's bedroom. This view shows the simple red window curtains which, though unhistorical, give the right feel. The Elizabethan portrait and carved chest are the only 'real' elements in the room.

STUART

1603 · 1660

WITH THE ACCESSION of James I in 1603, England's politically confrontational stance was replaced by a new spirit of pragmatism. James's dreams of European dynastic alliances paradoxically found their truest fulfilment in increasingly cosmopolitan artistic sensibilities. Well travelled collectors such as Thomas Howard, Earl of Arundel, brought back not only important paintings and sculptures from France and Italy, but introduced into this country the taste for arranging their artistic treasures in the manner of the great European princely collectors. Such internationalism was to bear its fullest fruit in the activities of those distinguished, aristocratic connoisseurs who formed an inner circle at the court of Charles I, aesthete, King and martyr.

It is against this backdrop of brilliant sophistication that we must view the remarkable innovations made in the arts of building and decoration in the years before the English Civil War. The single most important example of the new domestic architecture was the Queen's House, built by Inigo Jones at Greenwich in 1616-30, which showed how Italian Renaissance architectural principles could be made to work not only in grand palaces but also in the

The Kedderminster Library, Langley Marish, Buckinghamshire. In the seventeenth century books were precious and were therefore often kept under lock and key. Few book-presses were as beautifully ornamented as this architectural jewel. The cupboard doors are richly painted both inside and out; an effect which could be copied to good effect in any room with storage units or even a kitchen. The handsome chimney-piece with columns completes the ensemble.

rooms in which ordinary people lived.

For the first time there was a clearly defined set of rules governing all aspects of the internal arrangements of houses, arrangements which now found logical expression also in the design of the façade. The grand town house and the simple country villa developed simultaneously as distinct building types, but their interior detailing and decoration utilized a common language based on the classical tradition. Thus, every room came to be treated as a simple box, defined in proportion by these aesthetic canons and articulated by such applied details as chimney-pieces, door-frames and window-cases. The treatment of the wallspace in distinct areas, corresponding to the base, shaft and capital of the classical column, gave us the basic divisions which builders and decorators, often unwittingly, use to this day.

Rooms of any pretension continued to be panelled, and in the most opulent much of the woodwork was carved and enriched with gilding. Such high-fashion detailing was often imitated in paint, with panels of *trompe l'oeil* divided by real architraves, chair rails and skirting boards. This is a bold effect that can, with courage, be reproduced in a modern room. Where richness was not introduced by carving, it might be found in the exotic diversity of materials imitated in paint: porphyry, lapis lazuli and rare

The great staircase, Knole, Kent. This is one of the greatest Jacobean houses in England. Despite the scale of this staircase the noble effect of the now much restored grisaille *decoration of 1607-8 would adapt well to use in a smaller space. There is a clever contrast between the figurative panels,* trompe l'oeil *elements such as painted balustrading and the fossil marble finish used on the columns.*
The fine hall lantern is of a later period but entirely in character.

coloured marbles; and the dignified magnificence of ivory contrasted with ebony.

More fanciful schemes involved the use of pilasters, horizontal bands and whole panels of strapwork ornament cut out and applied to a darker or lighter field. Such decoration, as well as the characteristic shaped bannisters and other small applied details, can be re-created from plywood with a fretsaw, taking the patterns from authentic examples such as those to be seen on the great staircase at Knole in Kent. Fantastic elaboration is the keynote of decoration in this period, but simpler schemes are also possible. Indeed, the great majority of more modest houses retained the white-painted plaster walls characteristic of the previous generation, still the perfect foil to pictures of the period or textile hangings. Plain-coloured painted walls are rare; colour being associated, in decoration as in costume, with wealth and conspicuous consumption. This richness of effect can best be judged by looking at the jewel-like colouring and detail of contemporary portraiture.

The use of textiles in the Stuart interior remained straightforward. In keeping with wall hangings, curtain treatments were uncomplicated: lengths of silk or velvet, elaborated with braid edgings, were suspended by small rings from slender base-metal rods. Chairs with padded seats were only beginning to come in, while elaborately upholstered pieces remained the preserve, and the status symbol, of the grandee. All woven and figured fabrics were similarly an index of prestige, and the cushions which softened the chairs and benches in the simpler interior were of plain crimson velvet or more utilitarian, home-produced, woollen stuffs. The most typical chair of the period is the robust four-square type now known as the 'Cromwellian'. It is almost invariably upholstered in velvet, perhaps with a broad stripe and the edges finished with brass dome-headed nails or fringing.

Most of the furniture types thought of as characteristically 'Elizabethan' are in fact of the seventeenth century. The development of furniture styles is slower at this date than is generally supposed, and the introduction of comfortable seating came very late to most houses. Even at Knole, where many splendid examples of the period survive, the famous Knole Sofa was originally intended as a Chair of State rather than for general use. However, since it may fairly be described as the first comfortable seat in England, and has been endlessly copied since the nineteenth century, this sofa is, when dressed up with suitably grand tassels, the most workable solution for a room in this manner.

Of other fixed furnishings, chests of drawers began to replace simple lidded chests, just as heavy refectory tables and the convenient draw-leaf table on baluster legs superseded the cumbersome plank-and-trestle tables previously brought out and set up at mealtimes. At table most people still sat on small 'joint stools' or long, low benches, but for dining today, where comfort and convenience will be sought before authenticity, the Cromwellian chair is perhaps the answer.

In the seventeenth century the best bed and its textile hangings was the most valuable single item of

'The Earl of Dorset' by Isaac Oliver (1616). This portrait miniature of one of the richest and most powerful of James I's courtiers shows him as a military commander in his tent and is a definitive image of splendour on the move. All decoration at this date was to some extent flexible and temporary. Everything seen here, from the blue velvet draperies with bullion fringing to the fine turkey carpet laid over the matting, is lavish but portable. Note, too, the red velvet table-cover perhaps embroidered with Turkish work, here concealing a campaign table, but of the type which adorned even the finest pieces of furniture in grand houses.

Left: 'The Saltonstall Family' by David des Granges (1636). A scene in a well-to-do middle-class household. The red bed-hangings trimmed with a self-coloured border and fringe and the counterpane edged with lace indicate considerable prosperity.
*Above: **Lady Betty Germaine's dressing-room, Knole, Kent.** This modest private sitting-room must have been lined-out with oddments of panelling cut to fit. Note how the small pictures are hung grouped within the panels. The stools are in period but the chairs and dummy-boards date from the end of the century. The polished floorboards were originally scrubbed.*

the household contents. The finest examples were elaborately carved on the bed-head and posts, but it is the general box-like form created by the uprights and tester, from which the curtains hang, which creates the feel of the period. A modern four-poster bedstead, in a dark finish, is a good starting point, but an ingenious and flamboyantly theatrical effect can be achieved by suspending lavish draperies from concealed battens attached to the ceiling.

This is the first period in which it is no anachronism to lay a good oriental carpet on the floor. Rush and sisal matting are again sympathetic solutions to the dilemma of period accuracy. Wall-sconces for candles gained in popularity, but there were few other innovations in lighting in the first half of the century, and only in its latter decades did the illumination of rooms by spectacular fittings become a conspicuous form of ostentation.

RESTORATION

1660 · 1688

IT IS OF COURSE A MYTH that decoration, along with cakes and ale, was banned from the day of King Charles's execution. Puritan taste in decoration, as in dress, was by no means as austere as is customarily believed, and there was some degree of continuity between the styles of the old regime and the new Commonwealth. The return of the monarchy in 1660 was, however, marked by a revitalization of the arts and an exuberance in decoration, which reflected the optimism of a young king. Charles II's years of exile at the courts of Europe had given him a taste for magnificence, which was welcomed by loyalist families eager once again to assert their position through displays of grandeur. This ostentation was rapidly adopted by both the newly ennobled and the upwardly mobile. A typical product of the new era was Samuel Pepys, a clever and ambitious man on the make delighted to record the sums he lavished on dress and on the adornment of his house in the City of London. In the highest spheres, Court taste came increasingly to reflect the sensuous richness of the international Baroque style, and this influence percolated down through society, leading even provincial craftsmen to adopt a more lavish

The White Closet, Ham House, Surrey. The interiors of the Thames-side home of the Duke of Lauderdale are among the most important surviving from the late seventeenth century. This corner chimney-piece with its pretty marble slips and plain tiled interior is typical of small private sitting rooms of this date. The panelling with gilded mouldings frames a picture in the overmantel and this is flanked by candle sconces.

scale of detailing and an amplitude in the lines and forms of their ornament. The craftsman whose career most perfectly mirrored the decorative taste of his age was Grinling Gibbons (1648-1721). For all its miraculous multiplicity of natural forms – fruit, vegetables and foliage – his virtuoso wood-carving remains supremely architectural ornament.

Such prodigality of enrichment was always bounded by the same formal rules as those applied to English building. Thus the re-creation of rooms in the Restoration manner will start with those same divisions of the wall-space established by the introduction of classicism, but now delineated by newly fashionable, richer mouldings. Wainscotting gained in distinction by the innovation of the 'fielded panel' and the use of the new curvilinear bolection moulding which lent added nobility and a robust elegance typical of joiners' work of the age.

Textile hangings remained the smart alternative to wooden panelling, but enhanced now by the increasing sophistication with which they were tailored to fit the wall. The new practice of straining rich fabrics against a purpose-made framework of wooden battens superseded the old, rather haphazard hanging of tapestries and other materials. Effects based on the contrast of richly patterned silks and other colours and textures, such as velvets, were rendered more striking by the clearer lines of the taut fabrics, characteristically stitched into 'panes': that is, one panel of fabric set into a border of another, contrasting in colour or design. Similarly, windows and doors were framed with curtains of increasing elaboration, often finished with elaborate fringing and, for the first time, supplied with custom-made, co-ordinated tiebacks of trimmed fabric or rope and decorated with tassels. This was the moment at which that most French of decorative resources, *Passementerie*, entered the English repertoire. This application of braiding, fringing and tassels to all manner of textile furnishings rapidly multiplied the options available to decorators, permitting also the upgrading or updating of an existing scheme, making it then as

now a cornerstone of the decorator's art.

Strong colouring and dramatic contrasts marked the decorative palette of the Restoration. Crimson, purple and gold remained, by virtue of expense, indicative of prestige and were therefore redolent of grandeur. This taste for grandeur was as prevalent in paint treatments as in textiles, as may be seen at Ham House in Surrey, where wood-graining carried out over a gold-leaf ground echoes the richness of silk brocades. Marbling, too, played an essential role in the creation of the sumptuous interior, as conceived by connoisseurs who continued to derive their ideas of magnificence from Italian models; painted marbling continued to do duty for the real material until the influx at the end of the century of Roman and Florentine craftsmen working in *scagliola*. From the 1660s onwards, however, a native school of plasterers reached ever greater heights of virtuosity in the creation of ornamental ceilings; their special skill lay in the rendering of naturalistic fruit, flowers and garlands in deep-cut plasterwork.

From such ceilings hung chandeliers of previously unparalleled magnificence. These gorgeous confections, wrought for the richest of patrons by silversmiths whose ingenuity matched the imagination of the plasterer, are amongst the most dazzling manifestations of Restoration exuberance. The modern decorator can only hope to emulate this conspicuous display in the illumination of rooms by using nineteenth-century Sheffield or silver-plated wall-sconces in the Charles II style; these frequently very convincing replicas were made in considerable numbers and can still be found in pairs or larger sets, while their twentieth-century equivalents can also look convincing if their electric candles are removed. In the same way, it is possible to find acceptable substitutes for the characteristic light fittings of the more modest rooms of the period: Flemish chandeliers and wall-brackets in brass based on globular forms with simple curving branches, and more ordinary native wood or wrought-iron examples.

Fortunately, in furniture, as in light fittings, the

The Ante-chamber to the Queen's bedchamber, Ham House. *The magnificence of the decoration of Ham depended upon the richness of its textiles. Here the wall-hangings are brocaded silk 'paned' (bordered) with a different fabric further enriched with embroidery. The dado is equally splendid with wood-graining in black over gold-leaf. The furniture is mostly 'japanned' in imitation of real lacquer-work. Notice the oriental character of the screen and cabinet and the typical seventeenth-century grouping of a mirror and table flanked by candle-stands.*

Above left: Pictures hanging in the White Closet. The neat black ebony frames of these pictures exemplify the taste of the period. Such frames were used in tight groupings in conjunction with ribbons and bows, which disguised unsightly wires or chains and added one more element to the variety of textiles and trimmings.

Above right: Portière in the White Closet, Ham House. Many of the textiles at Ham were renewed during a campaign of restoration carried out by the Victoria & Albert Museum. This portière *or door-curtain demonstrates that it is possible to create a grand effect with cheap fabrics and tassels.*

Right: Door of the White Closet. This excellent example of wood graining in the extravagant seventeenth-century fashion illustrates well the way in which horizontal and vertical emphases combine to enhance the visual effect. Through the door is seen a chair with a vividly paned and fringed cushion.

le Blond excud auec Priuilege du Roy

Bosse in et fi.

nineteenth century's enthusiasm for the days of 'Good King Charles' has left a variety of good quality, suitably evocative pieces. The heavy, squat chairs of the earlier part of the seventeenth century had begun to evolve towards a lighter and more graceful form with a higher, ornamented back. These have always been much copied. Chests of drawers were becoming the standard type of furniture for storage, while at the upper end of the scale lacquered cabinets of Chinese or Japanese work, or English imitations, on elaborately carved stands enjoyed a vogue. The placing of furniture remained formal, though by this date rooms even in relatively modest houses had begun to be set aside for specific functions: for the first time we may distinguish the dining room, the drawing room and the study. Delftware pottery was favoured for both ornament and use and in particular those large pictorially decorated dishes called 'chargers' were displayed on the tops of cupboards or laid flat on tables. For its durability pewter was also popular, not only for plates and mugs but also for simple candlesticks. Pictures and prints also reflect the character and function of the rooms in which they hang. Thus images of fruit, flowers and game in the Dutch manner were considered appropriate for the dining room, while in the study individual predilections could be expressed either by pictures of religious or morally uplifting subjects or by luscious portraits of the beauties of the court of Charles II, according to taste.

Ladies Dining in a Chamber. Engraving by Abraham Bosse (c.1635-40). This convivial scene of a group of women dining without their husbands illustrates many of the decorative elements of the middle years of the century. Textiles predominate, with tapestry providing warmth and colour. It is treated as a simple wall covering with the pictures hung over it. Life centres on a roaring fire with massive baluster andirons (fire-dogs) on the hearth.

THE
ENGLISH BAROQUE
1688 · 1714

As the seventeenth century progressed, the taste for rich decorative effects and a consequent prodigality in the use of costly materials gave rise to interiors of unparalleled splendour in the royal palaces and in the houses of the nobility. The English gentry and merchant classes, too, increasingly found a new confidence and desire to spend money on domestic comforts such as upholstered chairs and on deliberate shows of modest ostentation in their homes. With the accession of William and Mary in 1689 and subsequently under Queen Anne, England entered into a European phase of political and artistic life, in which links with the Continent were increasingly influential in both spheres.

William of Orange's kingly aspirations, and in particular his rivalry with Louis XIV, called him to be fully aware of the value of court splendour. At the same time he brought to England, along with his love of gardens, a recognizably Dutch sense of the civilized life of the home. In these seemingly irreconcilable ideals may be discerned the beginnings of what is now regarded as a typically English characteristic: a sense of grandeur and ceremony within a framework of simple and well-ordered domesticity.

The Small Parlour, Beningbrough Hall, North Yorkshire. This room is similar in scale and purpose to the White Closet at Ham, but its corner chimney-piece is enriched with the newly fashionable bolection moulding in marble surmounted by a shallow overmantel leaving space above for one or more shelves for the display of blue-and-white china. Portrait engravings in thin black frames are grouped to enhance the architecture.

Throughout the period the influence of Sir Christopher Wren (1632-1723) and his circle held sway in all important architectural work. In the building of houses of any pretension a new balance was struck between the desire to impress and a feeling that well-ordered domesticity was aided, or was indeed the result of, a rational and careful disposition of the working elements of the building. Wren and other architects better known for domestic work, such as Sir Roger Pratt, gave their minds to the creation of new types of houses in which tremendous emphasis was laid upon these elements, including the provision of efficient fireplaces; large, easily operated windows providing light and ventilation; corridors and staircases to provide unobtrusive access to every room for servants; and, of course, improved sanitation. The classic houses of this new type, often called from the arrangement of the space a 'double pile', have commodious rooms, all of which open off a large entrance or stairhall. The best rooms are wainscoted and often further enriched with carved details and plasterwork. They are lit by tall sash windows (said to be a Dutch innovation) with numerous small rectangular panes divided by glazing bars which are noticeably thick in comparison with those of the later eighteenth century. Chimneypieces are often to be found placed diagonally across the corner of the room and, whether thus or centrally placed, are often adorned with an elaborate two-or three-tier structure incorporating a picture frame and a small horizontal panel of looking-glass. Both fire-dogs and simple basket-grates were in common use at this date.

The greatest exponent of the complex chimneypiece group and, indeed, the most important single figure in the creation of fine interiors in the late seventeenth century was the designer Daniel Marot, who had worked at Het Loo, William's palace in Holland, and who came to England at his behest to work at Hampton Court and elsewhere. Marot's style is one of great richness and complexity. It bears the marks of the continental baroque aesthetic in which every surface is decorated and in which costly materials and textiles are articulated into grandly conceived schemes. Marot's etchings give an excellent idea of the sumptuousness and density of detail at which he aimed. While conceived for the wealthiest and grandest of patrons, they had a strong influence on the decoration of rooms at all social levels; making, for example, elaborately carved chairs with exaggeratedly high backs popular in even quite provincial or rustic rooms by the end of the century.

Great prominence was given in rooms of the period to the use of textiles. Typically the walls might be 'paned' in two contrasting fabrics, or panels of a particular size in figured or cut velvet might be set within mouldings. Curtain treatments of the period reflect this quality of elaboration, with pelmets edged in fringed or tasselled gimps, from which hang layered dress curtains, often gathered in tiers of bunches, and either straight or pull-up working drapes. The most sought-after colours were dark and sumptuous, with dramatic contrasts such as black against red and the dazzling effect of metal-thread trimmings much in favour. Grand beds at this time represented the height of the upholsterer's art, with complex baroque canopies in which the carved forms were covered in fabric and surmounted by urns containing panaches (plumes) of ostrich feathers. In such a scheme the bed-curtains, covers and the seat-cushions of chairs in the bedroom would all have been decorated *en suite*. With a degree of theatrical extravagance it is possible to create something of the opulence of this look, especially if sufficient care, and some expense, is given to the *passementerie*. Look in particular for that classic trimming of the period, 'tabby fringing', a fringe composed of short alternating lengths of two or sometimes three different colours.

Floor treatments in the period remained simple. Bare boards were the staple, very occasionally stained. Matting was a relatively inexpensive solution in an era when indigenous carpet manufacture, like

Left: A Royal Bedchamber, etching by Daniel Marot (c.1695). Everything in this ideal design is of the greatest possible costliness and splendour and all en suite. *The bed itself is lavishly upholstered and a frieze of drapery runs around the top of the room from which fall festoons dividing the walls into panels. Particularly distinctive is the door surround with flouncing.*
Right: The Grotesque Room, Great Hundridge Manor, Buckinghamshire. The special feature which gave this room its name was the marvellous seventeenth-century paintwork in which architectural fantasies emerged from the swirls of the wood-graining. In this pre-war view the room is furnished with a mix of old and new things which evoke the spirit of Baroque decoration.

that of tapestry, was a luxury market reserved for the very grandest of patrons. However, by this date imports of Oriental or Middle Eastern rugs and carpets were beginning to make them less of a rarity, and by the turn of the century they were to be found in the rooms not merely of grandees but of country squires and city merchants.

The furniture of the last decades of the seventeenth century is marked by a baroque vigour and robustness of form, often coupled with the use of rich materials or strong colour, that give it a tremendous appeal. A number of the most popular types of furniture, which have now become standards, first came into existence at this time: the bureau-bookcase, the tall-boy, the wing-armchair and the tea-table; endlessly adapted by the dictates of fashion, they remain unchanged in their basic forms. At the top end of the market, and now virtually unobtainable, were the extraordinary pieces of furniture produced for the royal palaces: these were made in silver, boullework of brass and tortoiseshell inlay on a wooden carcass and a variety of other rare materials. The virtuoso skills of cabinet-makers were paraded in elaborate inlay and marquetry work; especially prized was a veneer technique in which matched roundels cut from laburnam wood were set in a repeating pattern called oyster inlay. Next in grandeur, and much reproduced in the earlier part of this century, was beautiful walnut furniture, while the most colourful (and perhaps today the most valued of the everyday furnishings of the period) were pieces finished in black, green and particularly scarlet lacquer, upon which were emblazoned chinoiserie designs of pagodas and mandarins in gilding over raised gesso. There are very good imitations of these lacquer wares made by firms such as Hille in the 1920s, and even today good examples of pastiche William and Mary chinoiserie are widely available.

A number of specific decorative objects can be used to give an unmistakable flavour of the period to an interior. Small rectangular looking-glasses in which the mirror has become dim, grey and sparkly should be framed in that characteristic, fat, bolection moulding that was favoured for panelling and other uses. Engravings displayed in ordered rows of plain black frames are, although strictly a fashion of the next generation, visually in keeping and more easily affordable than the small oil paintings such as Dutch landscapes in ripple-moulded black frames which look so right when hung quite densely and perhaps suspended on bows of broad silk ribbon.

Queen Mary's personal enthusiasm for blue and white china, either Oriental or the productions of the factories of Delft and their imitators, made arrangements of bowls and vases stacked on top of cabinets, on chimneypieces and over doors highly fashionable. Marot even designed a whole room in which all the decoration was composed of details made up of groups of small vases and other pieces of ceramic. The most evocative of all the ceramics of the period are the great tiered tulip pyramids in which cut flowers were displayed during the years following the so-called Tulipomania, when bulbs were imported from Holland by the thousand. This horticultural 'Big Bang' was an extraordinary and short-lived plenomenon during which spell-bound collectors and more cunning speculators ran up the price of single rare tulip bulbs to ridiculous heights. However, the passion for tulips survived the inevitable crash in this most artificial of markets and continued in both Holland and England well into the eighteenth century.

Following Mary's death in 1694 William ruled alone until he was succeeded by Anne in 1702. The 'Queen Anne style', especially in architectural terms, is to a great extent an invention of late nineteenth-century architects, designers and connoisseurs of the Aesthetic period. They took a few elements of the taste of the first decades of the eighteenth century and created a pastiche look composed of decorative clichés that we may recognize in the book illustrations of Walter Crane, Kate Greenaway and Randolph Caldecott, and which found their most convincing domestic expression in the 'artistic' London suburb of Bedford Park, Chiswick, which was laid out and built in the 1870s and 1880s. The style of decoration and furnishings under Queen Anne shows a clear continuity with what had been popular before the turn of the century, and reveals only a slow movement away from elongated and exaggerated forms, towards an even greater robustness and a gradual simplification in which may for the first time be discerned the solid qualities and rounded lines of the early Georgian era.

The Diogenes Room, Dyrham Park, near Bath. A grand, plain English room that hints at Continental Baroque taste. The stained wooden panelling frames tapestry that is bent to the will of the architecture, and provides also a sober foil to the rich gilded carving over the chimneypiece. A tulip-vase bears witness to the Dutch taste of the House of Orange.

EARLY GEORGIAN

1714 · 1740

'Georgian' is an elusive, if not evasive, term, much abused by antique dealers and the makers of dubious reproduction furnishings; and yet there remains a kernel of truth in such well-worn clichés as the 'Age of Elegance'. The styles of decoration and, in particular, the furniture types of the years from 1714 to the end of the eighteenth century, have remained for many the most influential of all the period styles; they represent the ideal of 'Englishness' as it has become understood all over the world.

In the previous century the precedent had been established, by the more adventurous and aesthetically inclined aristocratic families, of sending eldest sons on an extended Continental peregrination called the Grand Tour, which had graduated from an eccentricity and become an essential element in their education. Such men inherited, besides political and economic power, a tradition of patronage which enabled them to shape the visual taste of their contemporaries and the development of decorative art in England. The centre of this world of taste and influence and the man who, more than any other, shaped the rules that governed the architecture and domestic decoration of the reigns of the first two

A drawing room in Spitalfields, East London. This clever evocation of early eighteenth-century style was created in the last ten years within the shell of a house of 1720. The grander architectural elements such as the pilasters are salvage, whilst the 'carvings' are confected from real nuts glued together in swags and painted. Real candles in the chandelier give atmosphere and everywhere there are telling still lives.

Left: The Red Room, Chiswick House, West London. The formal character of this room for entertaining is reflected in the magnificence of its decoration. Note the monumental Palladian coffered ceiling and the richly gilded architectural detail of window, door and chimney-piece. Above: 'Shortly after the Marriage' by William Hogarth (1743). Hogarth's domestic drama reveals how grand Palladian rooms were actually used. In the background card-tables are set out for gambling with single candlesticks to supplement the grand silver chandelier.

Georges was Lord Burlington. He was himself an amateur architect of considerable talent but, more importantly, the patron of William Kent, an artist-craftsman who with Burlington's support became an architect and decorator of genius, perhaps the first in the modern sense of the word. The Kent-Burlington style, derived from the writings of the sixteenth-century Italian architect, Andrea Palladio, was massive, noble, Roman. This Palladian architecture relied, however, not upon sheer scale but upon perfection of proportion and detail. The exquisite villa built by Burlington at Chiswick, near London, encapsulates their ideals in a series of small but magnificent state rooms. In these rooms designed entirely for pleasure one may see the pure Palladian style at its most fashionable. The change wrought on English taste is a suppression of extravagant naturalistic forms in favour of no less elaborate but carefully controlled stylized classical detail. Once again such richness may seem impossible to realize today, and yet, paradoxically, this is the first English style for which all the elements – cornice mouldings, console brackets and other details modelled in plaster – may still be obtained from better suppliers.

Given these elements and using an appropriate figured silk on the walls, there is no reason why, provided that the space has reasonable basic proportions, you should not be able to evoke something of the quality of a Kentian room, an atmosphere at once grand yet livable, such as may be seen in the paintings of William Hogarth. Hogarth's pictures record not only the lives of the fashionable, rich and dissolute but also a broad spectrum of middle- and lower-class life. Study of these images reveals in particular the patterns of existence in rooms of the period and the way in which the furniture, which stood formally against the walls when not in use, was dragged out into impromptu groupings to suit the hour and the social occasion.

Inevitably the reception rooms of a middle-class house did not experience changes as radical or as responsive to fashion as the more whimsical and experimental manifestations of aristocratic taste. Between 1700 and the middle years of the eighteenth century neither the types of urban and provincial housing nor the architectural ordering and decoration of bourgeois homes changed fundamentally. Fully panelled rooms, either painted or grained, remained a solid symbol of material success. Such simple, rectilinear panelling, enlivened with bolection mouldings but carried out as at the time in inexpensive woods, could well prove cheaper as a wall covering than specially printed papers or woven silks. Much of the impact of such panelling depended upon clever finishes, but wood-graining is much less difficult than might be imagined. Starting over a base coat of a colour appropriate to the wood (many of which are available commercially, ready-mixed), the graining coat is brushed on and while still wet it is worked with combs and other implements such as

brushes or even a blunt stick, to simulate the natural grain of the wood. As with all the best paint finishes, the bold and theatrical will be more successful in creating a pleasing effect than the niggling attempt at verisimilitude.

The mystique of 'authentic' paint treatment, with all the mumbo-jumbo of pseudo-scientific analysis, should not deter even the amateur, for good taste will always count for more than paint scrapes in the successful evocation of historic colour. In the grandest schemes the convention was often employed of painting the woodwork and some other architectural details in a variety of close tones of the same stone colour to resemble masonry. Such schemes were also enlivened with gilding, and this must in all probability be the source for the use of flat-paint white-and-gold schemes, first popularized by Kent in the 1730s and never since out of fashion for grand drawing rooms and ballrooms.

Adventurous colouring was characteristic of the period, though paint technology lagged far behind the imagination of artists and architects. In particular, strength of colour diminished very rapidly as paint aged, so rooms were newly finished in dramatically enhanced shades such as brilliant blues, acid greens and candy pinks. These dramatic hues were applied as smoothly and evenly as possible, but the shortcomings of the paint made dense colours susceptible to streaking, a failing which has contributed to another of the paint mythologies: the idea that sponging and dragging are deliberate 'period effects' that one should attempt to reproduce.

The decoration of rooms of this period is characterized by a weighty formality, which is also reflected in the scale and propriety of the architectural features. The chimneypiece in particular expresses this sense of dignity. Ideally, it should be in one of two styles: the more voluptuously sculptural is in the form of a heavy but very narrow shelf supported on architectural jambs, sometimes scrolled brackets or consoles, or, in the finest examples, carved caryatid figures; the alternative is a crisply detailed surround in which

'John Bacon and his Family' by Arthur Devis (1742). The shallow architectural detailing of this room could well be recreated in trompe-l'oeil. *The furniture is a mixture of old and new pieces, the glazed bookcase being late seventeenth-century, while the sofa and armchairs, upholstered* en suite, *are in the latest style. The green baize table-cover might be a useful disguise for an ugly but practical table in your early Georgian library.*

The Painted Parlour, Canons Ashby, Northamptonshire. Strict and simple painted architecture lends distinction to a plain provincial room. The National Trust's sympathetic furnishing of this house is limited here to a solid gate-leg table, a good chimney-glass and a really fine fire-back. These elements, with the square of rush-matting and small rug upon the floor, are achievable within a sensible budget.

mouldings such as egg-and-dart enclose strips of finely figured and often colourful marble. In the typical middle-class room the chinmeypiece, like the doorcases and panelling, would usually have been made in an inexpensive wood, but painted to resemble a more fashionable, expensive material. In keeping with this sense of display, ceilings were divided by ornamented mouldings into formal and symmetrical compartments, each filled with the kind of classical conventionalized decorative elements, which can, again, still be bought.

The sash window of twelve panes which had become ever more fashionable in the previous half-century was by this date pretty well universal. While there is no demonstrable functional relationship between the new windows and innovations in curtain treatments, the lightness and clarity of design of the sash clearly encouraged upholsterers to create new and elegant curtain forms complementary both to the window and the other furnishings of the room. Perhaps the most popular in its time, and therefore the most evocative now, was the simple festoon curtain. The mechanics of such curtains were similar to those of their modern counterparts, so beloved of Sloane Rangers, but surviving examples show that the eighteenth-century curtain when let down hung flat across the window-case without profuse gathering. It was usually made of silk or a similar fabric and was unlined, so that when drawn up to the pelmet the bulk and shape of the festoon were governed by the size of the window. Both festoon blinds and simple straight curtains were hung from a flat, horizontal pelmet board often unadorned but for a finishing trim of braid or the curtain fabric. In grander houses, increasingly elaborate carved and gilded crestings were added to the board, giving rise to what we generically refer to as pelmets. Straight flounces or valances do occur, but great care must be taken in their proportion in relation to the window in order to avoid a Victorian or Edwardian feel.

From the grandest to the humblest houses floorboards were left unpolished, but were regularly scrubbed. In family rooms and bedrooms, carpets were employed to add warmth and a note of colour. Old Oriental rugs and Turkey-weave machine-made carpets are appropriate.

In furnishing a room of this period, you will find that it is by arranging pieces with the sparseness of the eighteenth century that the most authentic feel can be achieved. At the top end of the market the most characteristic pieces are the massive architectural, gilt or white-painted side-tables and formal chairs in the manner of William Kent. Single chairs by followers of Kent are today expensive collectors' items, and one often finds even the grandest dealers and auction rooms selling suites of furniture of which only parts are authentic. Since even these 'Harlequin sets' are vastly expensive, it is as well for aspiring Lord Burlingtons that the high regard in which the grand furniture of the 1730s was held more recently, from the 1880s to the 1930s, led to a thriving industry in the production of replicas. Many of these are excellent in form, though they benefit enormously from refinishing and re-upholstering. The same is true of the characteristic middle-class furniture types: the stout wing-armchair with ball-and-claw feet and the robust, cabriole-legged, brown wood chairs and small tables that always appear as props in the portraits of the period. This was the 'Age of Walnut', and prettily figured veneers of the wood made show-pieces of bureau-bookcases and slope-front writing desks. One piece of furniture with an unimpeachable pedigree is the small wine-table supported on a tripod foot. Sadly, endless reproduction has debased it to the level of a hopeless cliché.

Fortunately in this period the practice of framing prints in order to hang them on the wall became widespread, and so, for the first time, the use of engravings as decoration is accurate, rather than merely an expedient. Hogarth's prints, framed naturally in that slim black and gold moulding known to everyone as 'Hogarth', not only record the settings and manners of the times, but will aptly dress the walls of a modern evocation of the era.

MID·GEORGIAN

1740 · 1760

For all the pugnaciously, nationalistic sentiments expressed in many of Hogarth's paintings, English distaste for things French did not prevent artists and tastemakers from lifting that nation's artistic ideas. The influx of French painters and engravers into England in the late 1720s and early 1730s brought with it an increasing awareness of the fashionable French court style of art and decoration, which came to be called the Rococo.

Beginning as an enlargement of the vocabulary of decorative motifs considered suitable for the enrichment of rooms and of luxury artefacts, the Rococo had, by the 1740s, begun to subvert what was increasingly perceived as the arid formality of the Palladian ideal. The Rococo style had its origins in the decoration of imaginative and informal buildings such as garden grottoes and tea pavilions. Shells, artificial rock-work and vegetation, and exotic motifs drawn from Chinese and Gothic architecture all provided designers with inspiration for their richly varied ornamental schemes. The contrast lay therefore between formality and symmetry on the one hand and sweetly disordered asymmetry on the other.

With its overtones of frivolity and self-indulgence,

The State Dressing-Room, Nostell Priory, Yorkshire. In this house, famous for its superb Chippendale furnishings, we see how much the Chinese taste was a matter of applied detail. The magnificent bed upholstered in figured silk is basically neo-classical, as is the restrained chimney-piece, surmounted by an elaborately traceried gilt glass. However, the chief glory of the room is its Chinese export wallpaper trimmed with gilt fillets.

the Rococo style was inevitably seized upon by the rich and leisured as the perfect foil and background to a life of privileged amusement. Quite clearly this style expressed nothing of the aspirations and achievements of the solid burgher; but for a man like Horace Walpole it was a gift. There can be no doubt that Horace's 'little play-thing house', as he described Strawberry Hill, his pretty Gothick villa at Twickenham, Middlesex, near London was conceived as a deliberate rebellion against the Hanoverian taste of his father, Sir Robert, the great prime minister and builder of that ponderous Palladian pile, Houghton Hall in Norfolk.

Though Horace Walpole and his amateur architect friends spent many hours poring over old prints of real medieval buildings, the look they came up with had little authentic feel but a jolly and romantic quality, like a cardboard cut-out of a castle in a fairy-story. This makes 'Gothick' an approachable though challenging subject for re-creation. If you are ambitious to emulate this style, it is probably not because you have the architectural raw materials on site. There are very few houses, grand or modest, in the Gothick style, although it remained fashionable well into the nineteenth century. The most that you are likely to have to start with is a single associative window; or perhaps the fortuitous acquisition of a choice and spikily elegant chair.

It must be said that an attempt to impose the Gothick style on a sitting room will prove inconvenient and unsuccessful. It is the incidental spaces in a house, perhaps the entrance-hall or a library (if you have enough books to justify setting aside a room for one), that will best respond to such a theatrical treatment. Tall bookcases look particularly well

topped with Gothick arches and crenellated with fretwork battlements, but something similar could, with equal success and wit, be essayed in the bathroom or kitchen.

Architectural salvage is the immediate and obvious source for the pieces of Gothickry that will provide a starting point. Seek out lengths of carved Gothick moulding, arched panels (which often come from demolished churches), and, if you are very lucky, an eighteenth-century Gothick door or sash window with tracery. With such elements in hand, you must consider how the walls of the room should be articulated with these and other fabricated motifs. Highly evocative wall treatments of 'clustered columns' can be faked up using three or five lengths of dowelling to support real carved details, while simple cut-out arches can be greatly elaborated with painted or stencilled detailing to give a quirky, lively feel to the space. The eighteenth-century 'Goths' preferred to paint their woodwork in pale stone colours and off-whites, sometimes picking out details in tints such as pink or lilac-gray. On a simpler level, for those who seek only a hint of tracery, there are a number of commercially available wallpapers reprinted from authentic examples of the period. Horace Walpole had said, 'I do not intend my house to be so gothick as to preclude modern convenience', and he used many ordinary, commercially available carpets and fabrics at Strawberry Hill. The modern goth may do well to emulate this relaxed approach in the choice of fabrics and other elements, for simple small-scale printed chintzes often work better with gothick detailing than a relentlessly traceried expanse of drapery. Similarly, floor treatments were very plain; for example, bare boards or sisal matting with perhaps a

The Great Parlour, Strawberry Hill, Middlesex, by John Carter (1788). One of the plainer rooms in Horace Walpole's gothick castle; only the chimney-piece and a few pieces of furniture are actually gothick. Black and gold gothick looking-glasses may be out of the question, but you can obtain simple arch-back dining chairs, the rush-matting and gingham covers on the simple sofa and stained glass fragments for 'gothick gloom'.

square of Wilton-type carpet.

For the eighteenth-century person of sensibility the other style as rich in association and as exotic in effect was Chinoiserie. The elements of the Chinese taste derived their appeal not from the charms of distant history but from the fascination of distant lands. European travellers and merchants had, since the fifteenth century, returned from the Far East laden with exotic merchandise and yet more fanciful tales. It was the latter rather than the former that provided the inspiration for the European image of Cathay. In England the Chinese taste gained more general popularity in the 1740s through much the same channels as did the Gothick. Few authentic art objects or artefacts other than porcelain and some pieces of lacquer-work found their way into English interiors at this date. It was therefore through the medium of such fantastical and fragile erections as Chinese tea-pavilions that the style made its impact. Only with the more plentiful importation of the classic hand-painted, floral Chinese wallpapers, towards the middle of the century, did the style find more general favour and come to be used in drawing and bedrooms of more modest residences.

This is a look at once easy and difficult to achieve. You can still buy for a reasonable sum perfectly acceptable reproduction furniture in the eighteenth-century Chinese manner. This comes in two principal styles: classic 'Chinese Chippendale' and *faux-bamboo*. Chinese Chippendale furniture includes chairs with fretted backs, which go well with the archetypal occasional table standing on clustered legs and edged with fretwork galleries, and with those elaborately carved looking-glasses in which the painted or gilt frames burst out in a riot of rococo swirls topped with tiny Chinese pagodas. A good variety of *faux-bamboo* pieces is widely available even in department stores. Most of this furniture, while good in form, comes in unpleasant modern finishes. The bright gilding of mirror-frames will look well if toned down or even painted in a flat, rubbed greyish-green tone and, similarly, chairs of either the Chippendale type or in *faux-bamboo* can look remarkably good when finished in authentic Chinese colours like lacquer red or vivid greens.

The essential element in a wall treatment which aims to evoke this specific phase of the Chinese taste (rather than, say, the Brighton Pavilion look) is the wallpaper. At a price it is possible to buy papers which reproduce by hand-blocking something of the quality of the original Chinese artists' brushwork. But why not, like Lady Diana Cooper in the 1920s, paint your own? Unlikely as this proposal might sound, it is perfectly feasible – for anyone with basic graphic talents – to emulate the freely painted and often quite naïve trees, white and deep pink peonies and other luscious flowers and exotic birds which are staples of the genre. You might even consider a riot of tumbling eighteenth-century monkeys in homage to that charming eccentricity of taste known, perhaps because of its French origin, as *singerie* ('monkey business'). All this mad excess should be painted over a ground of simple flat emulsion in one of the colours used in the old papers: deep greenish-blue, ivory or buff.

Whether you opt for highly decorated walls or a plain colour, the Chinese taste does not call for pictures or framed prints. It is a profusion of oriental bowls and vases, massed on any available surface or proudly displayed on individual brackets,

The Print Room, The Vyne, Hampshire. A room much altered except for its classic arrangement of prints pasted to the walls with printed borders. The background for such rooms was sometimes white, but usually straw-coloured. The choice of subjects of the engravings, including Old Master pictures, portraits and topographical views was fairly standard in the period. Today you might use any prints that you have or reproductions.

'Sir Lawrence Dundas and his Grandson in the Pillar Room at 19, Arlington Street' by Johann Zoffany (1769). The real focus of this room is the collection of gilt-framed paintings, but the bright blue walls and reefed silk curtains, useful mahogany furniture and rich Turkey carpet make a handsome, masculine scheme.

which sets the scene and forms the perfect complement to the decorative ensemble. It is worth remembering, however, that by this date the mania for blue-and-white china had given way in the world of fashion to a new appreciation of the more delicate and colourful productions of the Chien Lung dynasty: the so-called *famille rose* and *famille verte* wares.

Similarly, incidental oil paintings or prints are not vital to the Gothick. However, since it is a style which relies heavily on historical association, this look can be enhanced by the introduction of historical portraits. Old, even bogus, oil paintings can work, but

perhaps the most telling solution would be to hang, in black frames, a series of the 'historic heads' by the engravers Houbraken and Vertue. These austere yet elegant images have a strong rococo flavour, imparted by their borders designed with flamboyance by those same emigré Frenchmen who had first introduced to English shores the alien but seductive frivolities of the new decoration.

Alongside these diversions, the mainstream of decoration in ordinary houses was informed by the abiding rules of classicism, and continued to advance slowly but without any momentous departures

'Colour treatment for a Georgian Room' by Edward J. Duveen, from **Colour in the Home** *(c.1920). An early and highly sympathetic Georgian-revival scheme for colouring the architectural elements of a mid-eighteenth century room. Duveen advocated seeking colour harmonies in nature, an unhistorical but successful idea.*

from the ideals of the earlier part of the century. This essential continuity is clearly visible in the room which forms the prosperous backdrop to Zoffany's famous portrait of Sir Lawrence Dundas, the cultivated collector seen seated foursquare among his treasures in his London house. This room epitomizes the virtues of good, plain Georgian taste. The most difficult elements to reproduce today would be the fine chimneypiece and the exceptional collection of gilt-framed Dutch pictures. The plain colour of the walls, here a characteristic duck-egg blue, and the masonry-white dado are as simple as can be to copy. Even the gilt fillet that trims the wall can be cobbled together from easily available picture-frame mouldings, while the furnishings, including stout chairs and tables, the Oriental carpet and heavy damask draperies are all quite ordinary. Though this room was decorated by Robert Adam it is sober and for its date, 1769, even old-fashioned; but it stands at the turn of a decade which saw the introduction of startling innovations in fashion and decoration, the consequence of a new internationalsim in taste among connoisseurs, artists and designers.

LATE GEORGIAN

1760 · 1790

IN THE HISTORY OF taste and decoration the late Georgian era is epitomized for many by the work of Robert Adam. Indeed, it might almost be said that the trajectory of this one designer's career coincided so exactly with the rise of neo-classical taste in Britain that his name is forever identified with 'a kind of revolution in the whole system of this useful and elegant art', that is, the art of interior decoration. The words are those of Adam himself and his brother James, writing in their monumental *Works in Architecture* (1773-8).

It is significant that the brothers Adam built very few houses or public buildings from the ground up; unlike, for example, the architect William Kent, who had worked during a period of extravagant house-building activity in town and country. In the first half of the century they were more often called upon to remodel existing houses, creating interiors in the latest fashion. Thus they were professionally closer to the modern concept of interior decorators than many of their rival practitioners.

The Adams were fortunate in that they made their formative Grand Tour to Italy at just the right moment, from 1754 to 1758, and yet more so to have

The Etruscan Room, Osterley Park House, Middlesex. Like Gothick, Chinoiserie and Print Rooms, Etruscan decoration was a fad of the Georgian age; Robert Adam's at Osterley is the finest. A duck-egg blue background contrasts with archaeological motifs such as urns and sphinxs in black and terracotta evoking Pompeii. The carved pelmets and white silk blinds may be copied quite simply, as can painting the chairs en suite *with the doorcases.*

returned to London – their imaginations fired by all that they had seen of both ancient and modern architecture and decoration at Rome – at a critical point in the transformation of the English house. A new, lighter, more archaeologically based and intellectual spirit in decoration was about to rout from the field of taste the massive and conventional ornamentation of gilded Palladianism. Beyond its grandeur of architectural effect and its elegance of proportions, the essence of the Adam style lies in the subtlety of its applied ornamentation. The vivacity and variety of this detailing were derived from the close study and careful drawings made by the Adam brothers and many other architects of late Roman stucco-work in particular. Surviving Roman buildings uncovered in the great programmes of archaeological research undertaken in the mid-eighteenth century at Pompeii and Herculaneaum proved an invaluable source for this new generation of designers.

The bastard offspring of the Adam chimney-piece and doorcase are with us still, in the form of debased products which are all too readily available from builders' merchants. The real challenge in recreating an Adam-style room is not to find merely a sufficient quantity of stick-on urns and swags, but to find examples of such details that are accurate in scale and well defined in their modelling, and to arrange them in a convincing way. Fortunately, casts of many of the favourite Adam motifs are still available, many of them made using the original carved wooden moulds, and, while inevitably more expensive than mass-produced examples, these make the most desirable, because they are the most accurate, starting point for a scheme.

At its simplest, and most self-conscious, the Adam period room is a simple box of good proportions with a handsome neo-classical chimney-piece. This might be of white marble with coloured or black and white inner slips, but such fine period examples are now hard to find and consequently very expensive. Painted wooden mantels were often used in middle-class houses in place of real marble. There are, today, a great many commercially available wooden chimney-pieces broadly in the Adam manner. Some of these are of the correct proportions and suitably enriched with details such as urns or corner *paterae*, but beware; many are hopelessly inept in their scale and form, as you will tell at a glance, and are covered with far too much badly moulded ornament.

The only correct forms of grate for the period are the dog-grate, raised to the height of a small chair on its own legs, or one of the newer forms of enclosed hob. Of these the finest are of polished steel and come with a fender *en suite*. This is also the era in which the cast-iron grate began to oust steel from popularity and, in its ornamentation, to become as important an element as the surround and mantel in the decorative effect of the chimney-piece.

Ornament is so central a feature of this style that it presents a challenge for the novice: not only must the profile of the ornament be crisp, but the density and precise disposition of the elements will determine the success of any period re-creation. It is therefore advisable to prepare the eye with a serious scrutiny of the design books of the period. Needless to say, the Roman splendours of Robert Adam's interiors, for example the one created for the Duke of Northumberland at Syon House in Isleworth near London, are unapproachable, but

'Mrs Congreve and her Family' by Philip Reinagle (1782). A comfortable mid-eighteenth century room to which the Congreves have added things over the years. The splat-back chairs are of the 1760s, but the oval gilt sconces and the satinwood table between the windows are up-to-date. The hob-grate is also new, but an older steel fender remains. The unpelmeted festoon blinds with matching blue cords have no trim.

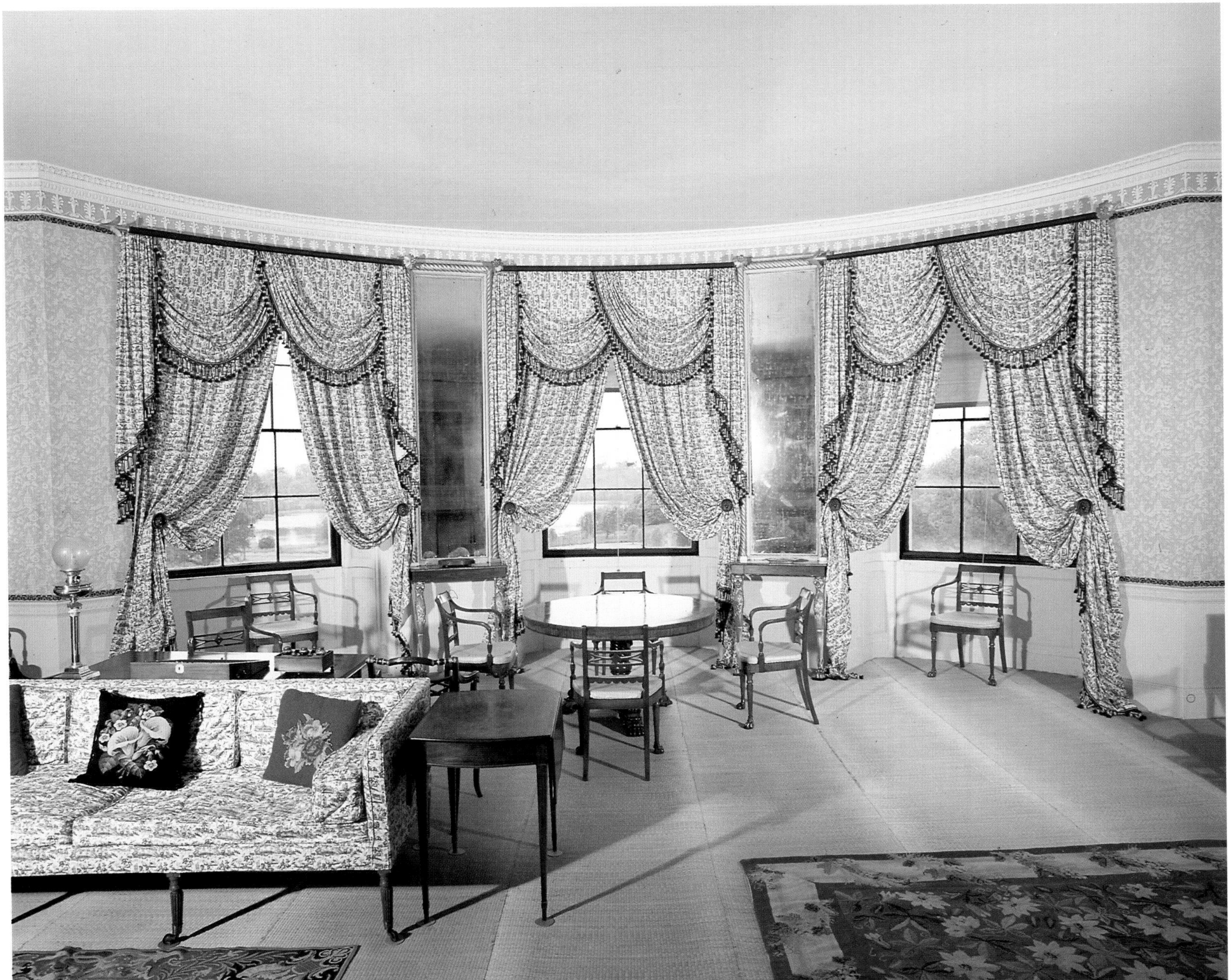

the underlying principles of taste and proportion make those rooms so magnificent can lend to the simplest of reception rooms an air of antique nobility. In an otherwise plain Georgian room such simple details as an enriched chair-rail placed at precisely the right height in proportion to the loftiness of the ceiling can make all the difference.

The choice of colours used in historic re-creation is always contentious, and no other period has been subjected to such scrutiny or suffered from so many wrong-headed attempts to capture what Osbert Lancaster so rightly called 'the fatal will-o'-the-wisp of period accuracy'. From the sickly schemes of the 1880s to the anaemic *eau-de-nil* and pale blue tints so beloved of the 1930s, decorators have, when re-creating late eighteenth-century effects, consistently failed to look at and take inspiration from the original architectural watercolours of the period. As the century progressed, house-painters were called upon to carry out increasingly sophisticated schemes of colouring. Subtle harmonies and often striking colour contrasts, such as deep turquoise and crushed raspberry pink, reflected and complemented the new intricacy of detail. Though it will be beyond most people's ambitions to install an Adam-style ceiling with painted compartments, the original designs for such ceilings provide an excellent starting point for the kinds of colour combinations popular at this time. Another readily accessible guide is to be found in eighteenth-century vases and domestic ceramic wares, upon which it is possible to see the colour harmonies used in all their original strength, undimmed by exposure to light and the passage of time.

At its grandest, the neo-classical architectural decorating style called for massive architectural furniture. Many of the rooms in this style were state rooms, used for formal occasions and fitted out with great benches supported on huge lions'-paw feet and tripod stands bearing *torchères*. Those who seek to fake-up a Grand Tour look, with classical urns and other archaeological trophies disposed upon a table-top wrought from a single massive slab of lapis lazuli, may these days have to set the horizons of their ambitions according to the grandeur of the stock at their local garden centre.

There are two simpler solutions to the problem of combining a degree of domestic comfort with allusions to the neo-classical ideal. The first of these is a Print Room, a form of decoration popularized first among connoisseurs in the 1750s, in which engravings of architectural and other subjects were pasted on the walls in formal arrangements, edged with printed borders and often further elaborated with decorative corner pieces, bows, swags or even printed and cut-out *trompe l'oeil* chains. The background colour of the prints varied, but in the eighteenth century straw-colour was the favourite, although white, red and other, stronger hues were also employed. A number of surviving Print Rooms are in houses owned by the English National Trust, who have most enterprisingly reprinted and marketed a useful range of the essential borders. A handy hint for those who lack a fine collection of Piranesi's etchings, or who, possessing them, not unnaturally do not wish to paste them irrevocably to the wall, is that good photocopies stained down with weak tea will pass muster.

The second and rather more ambitious alternative could be to attempt to emulate the charming Etruscan dressing room at Osterley Park House,

The Bow Room, Castle Coole, Co. Fermanagh. The highly elaborate draped curtains with their deep swags and bobble-fringe have been reconstructed in a Chinoiserie chintz reprinted from the evidence of an original surviving fragment found in the house. The National Trust market this and other 'document textiles'. The pier-glasses and pier-tables are part of a group of smart pieces of the 1780s including a sofa and a circular table.

Middlesex designed by Robert Adam in 1775. Here, a basically conventional room has been transformed with a novel form of decoration inspired by classical vases. Although the designs at Osterley were originally painted directly on the wall surface, there is no reason why you should not adapt the technique of a Print Room by cutting out prints for the main panels and, pasting them in position, join them up with free-hand swags and curlicues.

In all but the grandest and most fashionable interiors of the period, where gilt-wood chairs and console tables still held sway, the trend in furniture design was towards plainer and more attenuated forms which admirably suited the new and increasingly popular imported woods which began to reach England from as far afield as the Americas and even Africa. Most plentiful, and in a sense the classic late Georgian wood, was mahogany, much of which came from Honduras; originally used as a solid timber it came to be employed more often as a veneer, particularly as the most prized cut showing a 'flame' pattern in the grain grew rarer and more expensive. Good simple pieces of this period, such as the classic George III sideboard, are still plentiful, though examples which are useful in scale and of pleasing patina and colour command high prices.

Other exotic woods such as calamander and zebrana were used to enhance the decorative effects of finely made pieces, but the popularity of all these was far exceeded by that of satinwood, in which the pale coloration and subtle, shimmering grain particularly delighted the cabinet-makers of the age of Sheraton and Hepplewhite. Some of the finest satinwood furniture was decorated with painted swags of flowers, ornamental bows and panels of cupids and other pastoral or mythological scenes. Of such pieces, as of all Georgian furniture types, innumerable fakes, pastiches and honest reproductions exist. Some are atrocious, but many, such as those created by good craftsmen during the Edwardian period when enthusiasm for the late eighteenth-century style ran high, can be very acceptable, making it possible to build up the kind of coherent groups of pieces needed to create a room with the right feeling.

Perhaps at no other period since medieval times or until the 1960s did the richness of fabrics play so little part in the English interior. Plain silks and pretty printed cotton textiles very similar to the dress fabrics of the day were used, but heavier and more lavish materials seem to have been eschewed in favour of lighter effects more in keeping with the attenuated quality of much of the architectural detailing of the era.

In ordinary late eighteenth-century houses, including many quite substantial town houses as well as houses built in the country, there is a remarkable quality of reticence. The mouldings are thin; chair rails are often omitted; and other decorative motifs and conventional enrichments are used sparingly. Colours bordered on the dismal: snuff-colour and that grayish putty-like hue called drab were popular, while off-white and stone were colours used for door-frames, skirtings and other woodwork. Such deliberate plainness is associated with the lifestyle of those who espoused the new Non-Conformist religious beliefs; but there can be little doubt that this highly reticent taste is merely a more widespread, middle-class reflection of the chasteness of the contemporary neo-classical interior of high fashion.

'The Letter of Introduction' by David Wilkie (1813). Although painted in the Regency, this sketch shows an English room of the 1780s with furnishings in the French taste. The cylinder-top bureau has narrow metal trim following the rectilinear forms in the Louis XVI style. Note the simple octagonal pole-screen decorated with a print, the frame of seal-casts and the gilt trellis protecting the books in the bookcase.

REGENCY

1790 · 1830

O<small>F ALL</small> E<small>NGLISH</small> decorative styles, that to which we give the name Regency is the one most closely associated with the taste of one man: George, Prince of Wales, later the Prince Regent and from 1820 until his death in 1830, King George IV. The period covered by the term Regency has come to be applied not only to those years during which he was Regent for his mad father, George III, but more generally to the era during which the Prince's own passion for French taste and styles dominated the arts of decoration in England. Both the classical white-and-gold splendours of the Prince's reception rooms at Carlton House in London and the extravagant and richly coloured interiors of the Pavilion at Brighton contributed elements to the characteristic domestic decoration of the age.

French neo-classical architecture and decoration became, as early as the late 1780s, closely associated with the opposition party, the Whigs. These liberal grandees supported the Prince against the High Tories, and thus fashionable radicalism and stylistic innovation went hand in hand. A complete statement of this taste survives in the architecture and decoration of Southill Park, Bedfordshire, a house recast

The South Drawing Room, the Pavilion, Brighton, Sussex. The quintessential Regency fantasy composed of mad, exotic architectural features such as palm-tree columns. The pale walls are painted with flat gilt trellis patterns. Upholstery is an important element in the overall atmosphere of luxury, especially in the lavish drapery of the sofa alcove with its pleated back wall, tassels and fringes. Note the geometric pattern of the fitted carpet.

*Mrs Whitbread's Sitting Room, Southill Park,
Bedfordshire. A stylish French boudoir transposed to
the English countryside. The other end of this room is
curved, showing the influence of the latest French
neo-classical taste. The refined architectural
mouldings in black and gold contrast strongly with the
light wall-colour. The white marble chimney-piece was
brought from France and a fine chandelier completes
the fixtures. The furnishings too are ultra-fashionable
with a good gilt sofa and an elegant pair of pole-
screens. The upholstery and table-lamp are
Edwardian.*

for the Whitbread brewing family by Henry Holland,
a favourite architect of the Prince of Wales. The
interiors, executed by Frenchmen, illustrate the
grandest manner of early Regency, in which correct
architectural detailing and simple rectilinear forms
had their origins in the Louis XVI style. The resulting graphic clarity of such rooms became the ideal
foil to precise arrangements of fine French furniture, ormolu clocks and crystal chandeliers.

Such objects were of course far beyond the reach of
most people, yet for the first time these grand and
fashionable interiors became accessible to the middle
classes through the medium of books and periodicals
with coloured illustrations. In the plates of such
publications as Ackermann's *Repository of Arts*, one
may find illustrated examples of the grandest interiors and ideas for more practical schemes, achievable by the ingenious home decorator.

Most domestic architecture, however grand or
modest, remained within the broadest canons of
neo-classical taste. Thus the vocabulary of column
and pilaster, frieze and architrave continued to
provide a general framework, ornamented for the
first time with austere Greek details. Even in the
simple row-houses built by developers, this classical influence, derived from architectural pattern
books, remained the most important element in
their appearance, both inside and out. The single
most characteristic feature, therefore, of any
Regency interior is the architectural coherence of
the whole. In re-creating such rooms it is necessary
to observe the simple rules of applied decoration,
taking as a starting point those original features
which survive intact. Alternatively, the installation
of one new but historically accurate feature, such as
a good chimney-piece, can be the making of an
otherwise unpromising space.

The classic affordable Regency chimney-piece
consists of uprights or jambs decorated with simple
reeding, repeated on the horizontal member or
lintel. The corner elements are simple roundels; the
shelf above is typically narrow and also reeded along

'French Bed Chamber', from Ackermann's **Repository of Arts** *(1815). This is the kind of smart continental taste recommended by Rudolph Ackermann to his readers. This print shows a bed in the novel form of a Grecian couch. It stands in an alcove, its draperies supported on gilded spears. Note the alternative proposals for backing the bed with either mirror-glass or pleated silk and the possibility of fringing below the couch. The window curtains are held back by being twisted round the gilt cloak-pin tie-backs.*

its edge. The best period examples were of black or
white marble but, then as now, acceptable substitutes
of the same style came in pine, a wood invariably
intended to be painted. While the latter were originally made for bedrooms, there is no reason why
they should not be used today in a living room,
provided they are painted appropriately. Other
more monumental forms of chimney-piece were
current in the period, and these can be used with
success today, provided that their scale is suitable to
that of the room. Of equal importance to the final
effect is the restoration of the original cast-iron or
steel grate; if this does not survive a replacement can
usually be found. By this date the dog-grate had
been superseded by the more efficient, enclosed
hob-grate, while towards the end of the period these
were in turn replaced by the earliest examples of the
register-plate type, which was used throughout the
rest of the century. A good general guide is that
Regency models tend towards the rectilinear, with
relatively simple cast ornamentation.

The scale of the room must dictate the articulation
of the walls. In grander houses the wall will very
often be divided into the classic frieze, field and
dado. In more modest rooms, where there is insufficient height for a proper frieze, or indeed, a dado,
the wall treatment continues to the line of the ceiling
moulding. In such cases the Regency carpenter still
achieved a measure of elegance by judicious

*The drawing room, Knowle Cottage, Sidmouth,
Devon. A highly sophisticated, colour co-ordinated
scheme in a gothick cottage ornée. The ceiling and
frieze are papered with a* trompe l'oeil *trellis pattern,
the vines of which continue into the complementary
paper on the walls. The anthemion border also forms a
pelmet for the speckled curtains which hang in heavy
folds revealing the delightful vista beyond the bay.
Notice that the sabre-leg chair is upholstered in the
same fabric as the curtains, and that the latter match
the colour of the carpet.*

employment of crisp mouldings to doors and windows. To be in character, door furniture is best kept small in scale and simple in detail: a plain rectilinear rim-lock painted either black or the same colour as the door. Similarly, window locks and fittings should be modest and in plain finishes.

It follows from all this that colour will be the dominant element in successful evocations of the period. 'Regency stripes' in maroon and cream are best left in the suburban tea-rooms in which they originated. Stripes of any colour were rare as a wall treatment during this period but, used in unusual colour combinations and, in particular, if scaled-up and painted freehand, may create a charming effect. Patterned papers and flat-painted walls are equally authentic, the latter often being finished with simple stencilled borders, anthemions or Greek Key pattern for example. Ragging, dragging and sponging should be avoided – they all produce effects quite unlike those of the Regency decorators. They chose strong colours in sophisticated combinations; lilacs and sulphur yellows, emerald greens and crimsons, deep pinks, strong blues and gold. The faint-hearted, wary of such schemes, need only look to the glorious china produced by Coalport and other Regency factories to be convinced of the glamour and effectiveness of such counterpoints of colour.

Improvements in the technology of wallpaper printing brought pretty and reasonably well-printed papers within the means of the average middle-class consumer, making possible richer and more closely co-ordinated schemes, such as that of Mr Fish's celebrated *cottage orné* at Sidmouth in Devon. Contrary to popular belief, fitted carpeting was a desirable luxury. Few people can afford the indulgence of having a carpet like the one in the South Drawing Room of the Brighton Pavilion, Sussex, specially woven, but anything less fails the benchmark of authenticity. It is best, therefore, to be content with an old oriental carpet, a piece of Aubusson weave or acceptable modern substitutes.

Fabrics, used for curtains, upholstery or as a wall-covering, will form the secondary keynote of any room. Rich and closely woven cloths were preferred in this period: silks – plain, watered and taffeta; damasks for the most opulent of effects; and heavy woollen repps for more serviceable wear. The most spectacular curtain effects were often achieved with elaborate assymmetrical combinations of contrasting fabrics, further elaborated with fringes and tassels of silk or bullion thread. Designs that can be followed are to be found in the pages of Ackermann's *Repository* and specialist upholsterers' design manuals (a few of which have been reprinted).

The creation of authentic curtain effects has become much easier in recent years with the proliferation of good replica curtain poles and fittings: brackets, finials, rosettes, rings and all manner of tie-backs. Original examples, though eminently desirable, command huge prices, but a selection of modestly proportioned reproductions will achieve the all-important correct outline and form. The increasing sophistication of Regency decor dictates extra care in any modern reconstruction. A consciousness of the importance of design at that time, and continuing technical innovation, produced a wide variety of fittings, for curtains, lighting and other practical amenities, which one must emulate in as much minute detail as possible to assemble a coherent image.

A good central light fitting is one of the major statements in a room and should, therefore, be either original or the best replica that you can get. If you cannot find or afford a good one, have none. Since you should rely on table and wall-lighting to provide adequate, modern light levels, the central light is almost invariably best left unelectrified. Such ceiling pendants were at this date either crystal, glass or metal chandeliers or one of the great variety of oil-burning lamps. Gas was a rare and still dangerous novelty, found only in the homes of the grand and eccentric. In ordinary houses the simple candle continued to be the usual means of lighting, frequently enhanced in appearance by all manner of

H.Moses.del et sc.

'Drawing room furnishings', etching by Henry Moses from Thomas Hope's **Le Beau Monde**
*(c.1811). Thomas Hope's advanced urban taste is recorded in the plates of this little
style-manual. A fashionably dressed mother echoes in her draperies the asymmetric curtain
arrangement. The* néo-grec *furniture is massive in form and architectural in effect.*

shades, demonstrating the Regency love of things at once useful and pretty. Table oil-lamps came into general use in the period and these, when electrified, or their modern counterparts, work well as a practical modern lighting system, especially if they are wired into a centrally switched circuit. Dining rooms are a special case: there is still no substitute for the pleasure of eating by candlelight.

Regency furniture is expensive; good Regency furniture is astronomically expensive. You probably cannot afford to assemble complete groups of authentic pieces. Given that you may be able to put together three or four items at most, it is best to go for characteristic pieces with visual impact. In the drawing room, the priority should be to find a good single or double-ended sofa; in the dining room a set of decent sabre-legged chairs. Good Regency wardrobes can still be picked up as a starting point for furnishing the bedroom, but the ideal centrepiece would be a *lit-en-bateau* (good reproductions are now available) which, while liable to be expensive would be a worthwhile purchase. A plain modern divan, set along the wall and adorned with a drapery which falls from a central corona, will go some way to evoking that other delightful bed of the age: the *lit à la Polonaise*. Among the smaller types of furniture which add conviction to the *mis-en-scène* are pole fire-screens, small pedestal tables and single chairs.

The most characteristic Regency wood is mahogany, but ebonized pieces and those in the more exotic finishes such as lacquer and faux-bamboo effects all add to the rich mixture of colour and texture which makes the period so exciting.

Clarity of arrangement is the keynote for which to aim. The overall effect of the disposition of furniture and other objects should be, like the detailing of the fittings, architectural and even a little austere. Although the period saw the beginnings of informal furniture groupings, density or clutter must be avoided and the symmetrical placing of paired things remains the best way in which the rational style of Regency rooms may be evoked. Chairs may be free-standing, flanking a chimney-piece, but sofas were generally intended to stand against a wall, as evidenced by the inferior finish of their backs.

The placing of ornaments should begin and, in this period it might almost be said, end with the arrangement or garniture of the mantel-shelf. A clock flanked by candlesticks or better still a pair of lustres is the most obvious, but you can add small busts and other statuary, urns, vases, spill-holders and decorative porcelain. Tea and dinner services were never put on display; in the dining room the best silver would have been laid out on the table and the sideboard, but even then only on special occasions.

When it comes to picture hanging, those who have dashing Regency ancestors painted by Sir Thomas Lawrence will have no problem in achieving the right effect. The rest of us are obliged to be inventive. As in the earlier periods, prints offer an effective and affordable solution to the problem. There is an almost inexhaustible variety of black-and-white and coloured prints which are appropriate: other people's ancestors etched or in mezzotint, country house views and landscapes with or without sturdy squires engaged in slaughtering all manner of wild-life. Wild life of another kind is represented in the caricatures of Rowlandson, Gilray and Cruickshank depicting the follies and fashions of the age. Any or all of these, framed in simple mouldings such as the widely available 'Hogarth', can be hung in symmetrical patterns to good effect. The centrepiece of such a hang might well be a circular, convex mirror, its gilt frame ornamented with balls; this is one of the most evocative of all Regency objects, especially if you are fortunate enough to acquire one topped with an eagle or flanked by snakes supporting candle-sconces. The only other type of looking glass often found in ordinary Regency schemes is a chimney-glass. These can be a single large sheet framed in a suitable moulding, painted or gilt, or of the typical tripartite horizontal form. These invariably rest directly on the mantel-shelf rather than fly at half mast on the chimney-breast, so that they reflect the objects in front of them.

To embark on a full-blown scheme of decoration in one of the various exotic tastes of the period – Egyptian, Gothick or Chinoiserie – requires courage and a deep purse. For the enthusiast who owns even a single good piece of furniture in any of these styles, the venture is well worthwhile. Of the many novelties of the period, that most easily achieved is the tented room, inspired by the military campaigns of the Napoleonic era. Beyond this charming eccentricity which may be successfully contrived by anyone with plenty of fabric and a staple gun, the more lavish effects of a Brighton Pavilion will require, as George IV discovered, immense resources and the co-operation of a team of craftsmen of uncommon imagination and talent.

The Breakfast Room, Sir John Soane's Museum, London. Soane's grand and eccentric vision compresses more architecture into a small space than was achieved by any other designer. Note the use of convex mirrors in the dome and of narrow panels of mirror as pilasters, enhancing the vistas. Soane designed the handsome mahogany bookcases but the faux-bamboo chairs and pad-foot table are everyday Regency pieces.

WILLIAM IV AND THE YOUNG QUEEN VICTORIA

1830 · 1851

I F THE TRUE MILIEU of the Regency decorator, as of the Regency dandy, was the exclusive world of Society drawing rooms, then – by virtue of reaction – the upholsterers of the succeeding generation were most at home in the sitting room, furnishing the domestic hearths of happy families in that comfortable middle-class style known to Continental Europe as Biedermeier. The era of the Regency had been exciting both visually and historically, but it was an excitement which often verged upon the hysterical, shadowed as it was by the expansionist policies of Napoleon, which left all Europe exhausted by almost twenty years of war. Now with the nations at peace, people could once more travel, collect and cultivate the domestic arts.

The monumental classicism of the Regency continued to represent the patrician ideal of good taste; but it was the good taste of the State Room rather than of the family home. Increasingly, after 1830 ordinary middle-class houses tended to be decorated in a style which accorded as much importance to modern comfort as to ancient precedent. In the search for new forms for everyday household furnishings, designers and manufacturers shared with

The Games Room or Small Sitting Room, Stratfield Saye, Berkshire. At his country house the Duke of Wellington chose a domestic version of the newly fashionable rococo revival style for his reception rooms. A busy wallpaper sets the scene and invites an equally busy hang of small pictures and family miniatures. Elements typical of a new taste include the elaborate hanging oil-lamp and the heavy black marble chimney-piece.

their clients a fascination with novelty styles. In an age addicted to the romances of Walter Scott, with their fancy-dress settings, every designer was eager to raid the dressing-up box. Historic styles from Baronial and Renaissance through to what was conceived to be Louis XIV and Rococo came to be used in grand houses in complete historicizing schemes which inevitably found echoes in the furnishing of that new phenomenon, the surburban villa.

At the most famous address in England, No. 1. London (Apsley House), the Duke of Wellington showed his characteristic hauteur and judgement by commanding for the main rooms decorations in the rococo manner, because it was held to be the one style that could not be imitated cheaply; and this axiom certainly holds good today. Elsewhere in the house, such as the Iron Duke's simple bedroom, comfort and convenience barely exceeded that of his campaigning years. Many people today have, in modern flats, rooms as cramped and irregular as this, and it is cheering to see that such seemingly unpromising spaces can, when treated in the austere classical taste of the early nineteenth century, achieve a degree of period elegance and charm.

The reception rooms of the well-to-do middle-class home of the period are easily characterized: they are high-ceilinged, of ample square proportions and articulated with generous mouldings. Plasterwork cornices increased in elaboration and weight, with rich and increasingly naturalistic motifs of flowers and fruit echoing the central ceiling roses which the more elaborate light fittings of the day demanded. Similarly, the wooden mouldings of doorframes, dadoes and skirting boards became wider and flatter than their eighteenth-century counterparts and be-

gan, at least in houses erected by speculative builders, to display a certain coarseness in their profiles. At about this time too, in rooms of good proportion and height, the dado was often deliberately eliminated in favour of continuing the wall treatment down to a skirting, which consequently grew in height and complexity of profile.

Across these increasingly large expanses of wall the play of small-scale and finely detailed wallpaper patterns struck a new note of cosiness, and rapidly became the natural foil for a vastly increased density in all the elements contributing to the overall effect of a room. Grander rooms were still likely to have the wallpaper finished at the top, bottom and sometimes also the corners with a gilt wood or metal fillet, and this practice was reflected further down the scale in the use of printed paper borders. These were often very beautifully produced, especially (at this date) by French manufacturers, and their increasing use and popularity as an easy means of enriching a room led to a vast expansion of the wallpaper industry in the middle and later years of the nineteenth century. Today it is possible to choose from a wide selection of appropriate small-scale patterned papers, often with co-ordinating borders, reprinted from authentic examples. These are expensive. More affordable, yet still capable of approximating to the feel of the period, are the many commercially produced papers and borders available even in the high street.

Against these densely patterned papers was hung an ever larger number of ever smaller pictures. Small and increasingly detailed and brightly coloured oil paintings in rich gilt frames jostled with framed prints, portrait drawings and silhouettes. A variety of

The Duke of Wellington's bedroom, Apsley House, London. In contrast to the public splendours of the reception rooms of his London palace, 'No. 1 London', the Iron Duke retained in his bedroom all the austerity of his military days. He slept in a narrow campaign bed surmounted by the simplest of draperies hung from a plain corona. Plain walls are decorated with pictures merely propped up and the all-over carpet is clearly an off-cut from the grander rooms.

Colonel Northcliffe's study, Langton Hall, Yorkshire, Mary Ellen Best (1837-9).
The private sitting room of a retired military man, who had served under Wellington.
There is a plain dado surviving from an earlier scheme and an all-over patterned
paper edged with green borders. For the first time we see a comfortably padded sofa with
loose covers of striped linen.

hanging methods was in use at the time, of which the simplest was a single nail to support small pictures. Anything larger and heavier would be hung on wires or, in grander interiors, suspended from gilt chains; in either case these fixings depended from a brass or gilt-brass picture rod, held at the top of the wall at frieze height by brackets at frequent intervals. The appearance of pictures hung on chains or wires is a distinctive note which cannot be achieved by any other means; prints and other small works may, however, be hung on nails by little rings screwed to the upper edge of the back of the frame, so that the rings are visible against the wall, and this is also typical of picture-hanging at this date. Clusters of miniatures, customarily displayed in small black rectangular frames, and other small objects of family memorabilia filled other spaces, especially around the chimneypiece.

'Our Dining Room, York', by Mary Ellen Best (1838). A provincial room of the 1780s redecorated in 1837-8. The vertical pattern wallpaper is arsenic green, contrasting with heavy red drapery at the windows which have dark glazing bars. The brand-new dining chairs are the classic William IV model.

The hearth, long the symbol of home, increasingly became the focus of family life as well as the visual centre of the room. According to taste the chimneypiece might be either a great black or white edifice of marble or one of the light, frothy confections in the rococo style which look for all the world as though they were the creations of a demented pastry-cook. By this period the register-grate had become the standard type, complemented by an multiplying array of fire-making impedimenta and new forms of fender and guard. The mantel-shelf became deeper as it increasingly became the setting for permanent features, such as a clock under a glass dome, pairs of vases and candlesticks adorned with lustres. Equally evocative are those impromptu still-life groups formed of spill-holders, candle-shades and face-screens, which are so typical of the way of life of the age.

If there is one wood which characterizes William IV taste it is rosewood, or the imitation – in carefully executed graining – of its lustrous, deep reddish hue. It is visually a heavy wood with its black swirling grain, and in the furniture design of the period a similar ponderousness becomes apparent. The classical Grecian outlines which had delighted the denizens of fashion during the Regency gave way to a robustness of both form and ornament redolent of the Corinthian splendours of the late Roman Empire. Scrolled arms on dining chairs become more emphatic in their sweep; anthemions burgeon in ever more luxuriant form; and the profiles of pilasters become stylishly plump.

The centrepiece of any drawing-room arrangement should be a circular table, the most characteristic standing upon a single architectural column supported on a flat base with three bun feet or hairy lions' paws. Such tables were customarily draped, the fashionable paisley-pattern shawls adding a note of richness and busy detail to the 'tablescape' of society novels, Parian-ware figures or ships under glass domes. Facing the chimneypiece across the room could stand a monumental, architecturally detailed sofa, covered in woven horse-hair fabric or patterned velvet and replete with the heavily stuffed, fringed and tasselled bolsters and cushions into which the leisured middle classes loved to subside. Alternatively, should you be lucky enough to find a pair of these affable beasts, they will look splendid tethered either side of the hearth. For the drawing room, too, the period produced a number of furniture types dedicated to leisure. Little tables with adjustable bookstands proliferated, while all manner of work-boxes and other pieces associated with polite pastimes such as embroidery and painting in watercolours were dotted about the room. Those useful wooden racks called Canterburys, originally intended for sheet-music, have found today a new lease of life as a means of preventing the ever-rising tide of glossy magazines from overwhelming your nicely judged period effects.

Left: A breakfast room, London. This room in a fine terrace house of the 1840s, decorated in the 1960s, creates with its rosewood overmantel and terracotta walls a characteristically masculine ambience. The collection of reproductions of Greek vases evokes an academic taste for the ancient world married to a thoroughly nineteenth-century love of opulence. Coloured glass in the side panels of the French doors is an authentic detail. The curtain treatment is the only softer and more feminine note, with delicate draperies, edged in elaborate fringing, suspended from a massive gilt pole.

Above: The shelves in this room were designed and made by the owner; a piece of Do-It-Yourself based on Thomas Hope's vase room, as illustrated in a plate from the book of designs of his Duchess Street mansion (1807). This detail from a Regency pattern book hints at the continuity of the classical tradition and provides an authentic touch.

The colouring of the drawing room, the room which normally reflects most closely the prevailing fashion, was at this time enlivened by wallpapers and textiles manufactured using new chemical-based dyes. The virulent green of poison-ivy, sharp yellows, bright crimsons and saturated brilliant blues all appeared for the first time in the decorative palette of the ordinary middle-class home. This new brilliance of colour was manifested in both carpets, which tended towards ever denser and more naturalistic ornament, and curtains. As in the Regency period, drawing-room curtains were the most elaborate: the plain wool working curtains often being supplemented by 'dress-curtains' of rich brocaded silks or brocatelles, which hung undisturbed in their precise folds, held back by ropes or flat tie-backs secured to massive ormolu rosette-headed pins or by leaf- or scroll-shaped fitments. Elaborate headings composed of swags and fish-tails continued in fashion, though by this date the complicated edgings of the early years of the century were giving way to simpler, heavier fringing. The innovation of the 1830s was the flat fabric pelmet, which at first backed an arrangement of swags, but later became a self-sufficient element concealing the mechanism for drawing the curtains.

As that arbiter of nineteenth-century taste, Mrs Haweis, remarked: 'the best ornament for a dining room is a well-cooked dinner'; but a matched set of William IV chairs and a handsome sideboard run this a pretty good second. The classic sideboard of the period is a veritable temple to the art of hospitality: it stands upon two massive pedestals and is fitted out with cupboards and drawers for bottles, cutlery, and all the impedimenta of stylish dining. Some examples still retain the brass rail at the back, upon which a gathered silk flounce hung to protect the wall covering from splashes when serving food. This little curtain forms the perfect backdrop to an arrangement, when the room is in use, of silver, or silver-plate tureens and domed dish-covers and decanters standing in coasters. Traditionally, the essential character of nineteenth-century dining rooms was masculine, contrasting with the more feminine quality of the drawing-room decorations. Etruscan reds, deep greens, terracotta and other browns were the sombre colours considered suitable. Pictures, too, tended towards the lugubrious; generally these were only oil paintings in heavy gilt frames, and the preferred subjects seldom strayed far from family portraits, pictures of animals and still-lifes of game and fruit. By this date the accepted domestic wisdom dictated that no superfluous textiles which would retain the smell of food should be used in the dining-room. Curtain treatments were kept simpler than elsewhere in the house, with plain but heavy drapes of felt, repp or mohair velvet, while carpets, either close-fitted or in squares, were chosen with serviceable all-over patterns.

Not all dining rooms had this 'Brown Windsor soup' atmosphere; some suggested a more cultured world as they became the repository of collectors' treasures such as those high-quality nineteenth-century replicas of Greek vases. This type of scheme is, in comparison with the conventional mainstream of decoration in this era, a mild academic eccentricity. It reminds us nevertheless of the continuing importance to this date of the great classical tradition which had since the time of Lord Burlington (see page 47) inspired so many noble schemes.

'Past and Present: 1' by Augustus Leopold Egg (1858). A bourgeois drawing room which stands at the point of transition from early to high Victorian taste. The rococo revival overmantel glass and the simple garniture with a carriage clock look back to the 1830s, but the rusty crimson wallpaper, probably flocked, and the plush draped centre table speak of the high tide of nineteenth-century middle-class taste.

HIGH VICTORIAN

1851 · 1870

Q ueen victoria, who came to the throne in 1837 and reigned until 1901, gave her name to a period as long and eventful as, for example, the era from the General Strike of 1926 until the present day. It embraced, inevitably, both major changes in taste and constant fluctuations of fashion. That convenient word, Victorian, thus applies equally to the rococo revival of the frivolous 1830s and to the aesthetic experiments of the 1890s in the *Art Nouveau* manner. However, the decorating style with which the Victorian era is most closely associated in the popular imagination is that which received its

impetus in 1851 from the Great Exhibition in Hyde Park, London, and continued, in greater or lesser degree, to influence the look of the middle-class home until the First World War and beyond.

At its grandest, this taste was closely allied to the splendours of decoration in France under the Second Empire; at its simplest, it was circumscribed by the purse of the average clerk. It is the style of great London palaces and of the Pooters' suburban sitting room immortalized by George and Wheedon Grossmith in their classic *Diary of a Nobody* (1894). The elements uniting these various dwellings are

A drawing room chimneypiece, London. This white marble chimneypiece with its archetypal black-leaded grate forms the centre-piece of an ornate drawing room, decorated during the 1960s as a homage to high Victorian taste. Some elements such as the naturalistically painted plasterwork are exactly in period for the 1860s; the modern gold watered-silk wallpaper suggests a similar opulence.

The drawing room, 5, Cheyne Row, London. The National Trust today preserves Carlyle's house, retaining the spirit of an intellectual household of the mid-century. The wallpaper is Morris's famous and still-printed "Willow" pattern. The carpet is a square of large classical pattern, probably sewn from strips. The furniture is generally old-fashioned but the scrap-screen adds an appropriately literary touch.

easily identifiable, and make High Victorian probably the easiest period look of all to recreate. Anyone who owns a house or flat put up in the second half of the nineteenth century, and in which the majority of the original details survive, already has the bones of a High Victorian room. The extent of the building stock of this era is huge, for British cities experienced in the 1850s, 1860s and 1870s an unprecedented building boom exceeded only by the vast ribbon developments of the 1920s and 1930s.

Throughout the High Victorian period, classical principles continued to be applied to most domestic interiors. The exterior design and applied decorative details of the average suburban villa might owe as much to the revived enthusiasm for Gothic architecture, but this had relatively little impact on the ordering of a living room. Examples do exist of houses carried out entirely in the Gothic taste, one of

'The dining room, 5, Cheyne Row, London' by Robert Tait (1857). *The historian, Thomas Carlyle and his wife in the front dining room of their Chelsea house, a classic example of the English nineteenth century arrangement of interconnecting rooms divided by high double doors. Note how these fold back against the walls. Above the eighteenth-century dado there is a small patterned paper, hung in 1853, with a narrow rope border.*

the most remarkable being the Tower House built in Kensington, London, by the architect William Burges, for his own use. To live cheek-by-jowl with riotous stencilled arcading and gilded friezes out of an illuminated manuscript required, however, a single-mindedness beyond any but the most restless of imaginations.

Most houses built in the second half of the nineteenth century were fitted with standard cornices derived from classical models. Similarly, most rooms would have had a wooden dado rail with a different decoration below and above it and a frieze round the top of the wall, or else wallpapers or paints alone would have defined the divisions of the walls. Picture rails are almost always a later addition and are best removed: they give an early twentieth-century feel to any room. The dense and symmetrical patterns of gilt-framed oil paintings, water-colours and elaborate prints favoured at the time were hung, in grander rooms, on chains or gilt-brass picture wire from picture rods supported on brackets at frieze level. In humbler rooms the pictures were hung directly on hooks or nails driven into the wall.

Chimney-pieces and grates define this mid-century look most exactly. The marble or wooden chimney-piece of the early Victorian era was still the norm, though the weight and depth of the mantel shelf gradually increased to accommodate the more elaborate garnitures which became fashionable as the century wore on. The arch-topped register-grate was universal, and its solid unbroken sweep, like the entrance to one of Brunel's railway tunnels, is absolutely characteristic of the age. Throughout the period, too, the impedimenta of the hearth – pokers, tongs, brushes and the various forms of coal scuttle or *purdonium* – increased in elaboration, and fenders, which had previously tended to be relatively plain, grew correspondingly ornate.

The single most significant advance in decoration was the rise to fashion of painted architectural ornament, usually stencilled and often applied in conjunction with wallpaper above the dado line. Wallcoverings at the grandest extreme of fashion continued to include silk stretched over battens, and the drawing rooms and ballrooms of Mayfair wallowed in overwrought damasks. Up above, these great reception rooms would be picked out in naturalistic colours, so that the plaster ceilings seemed heavy with garlands of hothouse flowers and fruits. The field, or surface, of the ceiling might be enriched with applied decoration stencilled in gold and rich polychromy. The stencilling might also, where silks or printed papers were not used, extend the motifs from the ceiling down the walls, defining the architectural detailing of the room. Painted decoration has the great advantage that it may be used for both the grandest public buildings – the most striking surviving schemes being those in the Palace of Westminster – or for relatively modest rooms. It can take the place of expensive plaster-work or moulded detail, and it lends, in every case, a very particular and characteristic richness of effect.

Wallpaper was by this date widely available, through commercial mass-production, in an extraordinary variety of patterns. Not all of it was of good quality, and the woodblock-printed papers of the Arts and Crafts Movement (discussed in the next chapter) were an example of the reaction against poor roller-printed papers in which the colours were harsh and definition uncertain. Some firms, however, produced magnificent patterns and many of these are once more available as 'document' reprints; one of the best sources is Watts & Co, still working today from their original hand-cut woodblocks. Coles, too, produce to order some of their characteristic nineteenth-century papers and printed borders. Simple floral patterns of the kind used in the parlour of the Carlyles' house in Chelsea are typical of taste in the mid-Victorian era. This room, one of the most liveable and evocative domestic interiors recorded from this time, is an ideal model for reconstruction. By contrast, the grander and increasingly geometric patterns of later Watts papers evoke precisely the massive, architectural quality of many 'up-market' rooms of the 1870s and early 1880s. Versions of the embossed papers of the period, often erroneously lumped together under

A bedroom, Osborne House, Isle of Wight. An elephantine bed with a half-tester, draped entirely in chintz and heavily fringed, dominates this royal bedchamber. Ranks of gloomy religious pictures are a little enlivened by the pale green moiré paper. Note the bed-step, to the right of the bed, embroidered with Bargello work and the fine Indian ivory dressing set to the left. The low chimneypiece is characteristic of the date.

The Drawing Room, Calke Abbey, Derbyshire. *An earlier room given its main character by an early nineteenth-century chimney piece, pier-glasses and suite of chairs and sofas. By the mid-nineteenth century the addition of occasional chairs, small tables and their attendant ornaments had given the room that distinctive quality which derives from the density of furnishing that satisfied the high Victorian eye. Note the Parian china figures and clock.*

the old trade names 'Lincrusta' and 'Anaglypta', are still produced, but these should be used with caution, observing the simple (but all too often overlooked) rule that ceiling or dado patterns should be used only for their proper purpose. These embossed papers were always painted, in darker shades for the dado and in mid-tones for ceilings.

In spite of research and the many books which have appeared on the subject, it remains a widely held misconception that Victorian rooms, whether early, mid or late, were muddy or dusty in colour. This is partly the result of a folk memory of the generation which grew up in the 1920s, reacting against the decoration of the drawing rooms and parlours of maiden aunts, and partly the result of hasty aesthetic judgement passed on surviving interiors. In both cases the first error has been to make insufficient allowance for the effects of sun and age, of the grime of coal fires and frequent city fogs of the period. Then, too, one must allow for the effects of light on fugitive dyes and the general decay of paper and textiles over the years. In fact, the chief note struck by the Victorian interior tended to be one of sombre but colourful richness. Earth colours such as deep browns, terracottas and rusty reds were much favoured, but were often enlivened with gold, yellows and black outlining or stencilling. Imperial purple, again enlivened with gold, was a popular colour for grand schemes, along with blues from indigo through Prussian to deep azure. Strength of colour is essential for the High Victorian interior. Though light was of course largely excluded, because of its destructive effect on the materials of decoration and the surfaces of furnishings, the strong palette of the Victorian decorator made rooms glow with a deep and lustrous richness.

By the mid-1840s the 'upholder' or upholsterer of the eighteenth-century and Regency period had developed into a general supplier who might also make up curtains and loose covers to the client's order, as well as fit out rooms completely, using a team of appropriate craftsmen. The growth of such

firms was a major influence on taste in decoration, not so much in the sense of the cultish individuality of the twentieth-century decorator, but rather in the quiet influence of the retailer, whose stock and working methods defined the choices available. Crace, though larger and better known than many, was typical of the firms of the period in that they commissioned fabrics, made furniture and employed a host of craftsmen who executed every detail of a vast scheme of decoration. This kind of attention to detail, from general concept to the last brass doorplate, was pervasive; it can be seen at its grandest and most effective in the sequence of rooms carried out in the 1870s at Longleat in Wiltshire, where every element, including the original textiles, survives intact.

Curtains were generally hung from poles. Brass poles of at least 2in (5cm) in diameter add to the opulence of a room, but a wooden pole, again of sufficient scale, will do quite well. Wooden poles were sometimes painted gold or finished in effects such as rosewood graining to give an impression of opulence. All poles should be supported on the proper brackets, many of which have a decorative rosette which forms the head of the screw securing the pole. These often echo the form of 'cloak pin' tie-backs and are, along with the elaborate finials of the pole, essential elements in the composition of the window treatment.

This was the era of the bay window, either swept in a single curving 'bow', or breaking forward to form a three-sided polygonal addition to the floor-plan. Depending on the size of the bay, it is equally correct to curtain it either round the line of the windows or straight across the beam. The latter is certainly easier with a curving bay, since otherwise you must find or commission and have made-up a swept pole to match the exact curve of your window. Appropriate curtain fabrics are silks for the grandest drawing rooms, and cut or plain velvets, mohair or felt, the last used only in dining rooms. Floral prints, or 'cretonnes', were used chiefly in the bedroom, or in some cases as summer curtains and loose covers. Straight, flat pelmets came into vogue during the period, and curtains were generally hung in straight drops, caught back by brass or, grandest of all, gilt-bronze (ormolu) tie-backs of pin or loop form attached to the outer edge of the window-frame or shutter-cases. Border trims were generally used, sometimes made from a contrasting fabric or from ribbon, strips of embroidery or tapestry, but most often from special braids, many of which were fringed or tasselled. The use of two borders, one broader and applied at skirting-board level, the other narrower and a little higher, was typical; though the degree of elaboration of such *passementerie* depended on the scale of the room and the nature of the curtain treatment.

Lace curtains became almost universal in the second half of the century. The authentic material for the best lace curtains is Swiss lace on a voile backing. The more usual, still readily available and affordable alternative is machine-made heavy lace – generically still called Nottingham lace after the principal centre of manufacture. It came, like its grander cousin, in panels, and the pieces, which can be bought either second-hand or new today, must be hung in pairs. A convenient trick with smaller windows is to split a single panel vertically and use the two halves border edge to border edge. Single curtains gathered and draped across the sash are typical only of suburban windows of the present century. In the nineteenth century most rooms of any decorative pretensions at all had blinds in addition to curtains. Modern roller blinds in cream cloth give a simple but accurate effect, while Lincoln green looks very well in a library, and plum or deep red will give a club-like atmosphere suited to a billiard-room. Blinds in a drawing room and, more particularly, in a bedroom, may be finished with a lace trim along the bottom edge. The blind cord must be fitted with a wooden 'acorn', not an ugly modern pull made of plastic, inevitably moulded in a 1950s profile.

Fitted carpeting was used, but more popular, at least in the 1870s and 1880s, were machine-woven carpets in the French taste or copied from oriental patterns. Fortunately many survive, and it is often possible to buy a good 'body-and-border' machine-made carpet of the period at auction. Several surviving firms still weave patterns from their archives and will also make up special orders if the relevant pattern cards still exist. Turkey carpet in the bold red and blue patterns favoured in the latter part of the century frequently turn up in sales or even in second-hand shops and markets, and are particularly effective for evoking the right atmosphere for a dining room or study. Machine-woven Aubusson and Savonnerie-type patterns are ideal for the drawing room or boudoir, especially in lighter colours, considered during the period to be appropriate to the female preserve. Floor boards were generally stained or painted dark brown.

The formal and informal variations in room arrangements may be seen in many contemporary paintings and archive illustrations. The choice of furniture is wide, and much solid, mass-produced furniture of the era is still available. In a drawing room, 'balloon back' occasional chairs, and sofas and armchairs with deep buttoned upholstery in silks are typical, though early Victorian neo-classical pieces can be used to great effect. The classic arrangement of the mid-century room focused on a centrally placed circular table, often draped with a rich cloth; a paisley shawl looks ideal.

In the rooms of the comfortable bourgeois, side-tables abounded, frequently elaborately carved and often provided with two or more tiers for the display of decorative objects. Opulence of silhouette and infinite elaboration of detail were the desired effects in the drawing room. Simple guidelines may be followed in selecting appropriate pieces, for at no other time in the history of the English house were the furnishings and their use more regimented: thus, the drawing room of the upper classes and the parlour of the lower middle classes were equally rigorously reserved for formal sitting, and only furniture appropriate to ornament or entertain-

A Library, London. This room in an artist's studio house of the 1860s depends for its distinguished effect upon the vast scale of the fitted library bookcases, bought from a country house sale, and the profusion of antique textiles, some by William Morris, which are used throughout the room. A panther skin rug on the floor breaks up the huge expanse of patterned carpet.

ment was to be used in these rooms. In the dining room a table, chairs and serving furniture such as a sideboard were the functional and necessary fittings. Chests of drawers were found only in bedrooms or on upper landings, where they naturally served these areas, storing clothes and linen. Such simple rules defined every aspect of life in a Victorian house.

The practical servicing of such houses increased greatly in sophistication, and one may speak for the first time of the technology of the domestic world. In re-creating period interiors there will be limitations on the degree of authenticity desired, particularly in kitchens and bathrooms.

Bathrooms can be replicated without too much

Above: The Kitchen, Saltram House, Devon. Within a building of 1788 this kitchen exhibits all the elements one might expect to find at any date in the nineteenth century. It is tied only to the middle decades by the black-leaded range, which had superceded the older spit, to be seen above the old fireplace.
Right: Victorian Bathroom, reconstruction at the Science Museum, London. Ceramic tiling is the keynote in the decoration and fitting-out of the nineteenth-century bathroom. Technical innovations include the flushing lavatory and piped water and drainage. The aim was hygiene coupled with high style.

difficulty for the latter part of the century, since original fittings can still be found, and many accurate reproductions have recently come on the market to meet a growing demand. Special care should be taken with wall treatments: tiles were used much less extensively than today (or than is popularly imagined of the nineteenth century), and tongued-and-grooved boarding, up to dado height and usually painted, was characteristic of many middle-class bathrooms. Flooring in houses where marble, mosaic or terazzo was too expensive an option was generally of figured or marbled linoleum. Kitchens were large, often occupying the basement of the house. If you have a kitchen of this size, it is quite

possible to fit it out with the correct kind of painted wooden cupboards, consisting of base units with solid doors below a row of drawers, and wall-hung open shelf units and glass-fronted cabinets for glass and other china. In grander houses dressers carried the workaday crockery used below stairs, but the cottage-style dresser laden with pretty ironstone and lustre tableware is a rare instance of a nostalgic cliché being accurate, for such dressers certainly looked like this, especially in the country where the farm-house kitchen was the focus of daily life.

Lighting technology made rapid advances in urban areas in this era, but outside the cities remained unchanged until the end of the century and beyond. Gas was widely used by the 1850s and brought some specific new fitting types to the home, but the wide variety of oil-burning lamps remained the preferred lighting for many until late in the century. Oil or candle-power provided almost all the lighting for houses in the country until the moment when the first avant-garde owners of grand houses, such as the Duke of Rutland at Belvoir, installed electric lights. In re-creating the feel of the period, electrified oil-lamps may be recommended as the simplest and most effective solution to the problem.

The variety of styles of the second half of the century which can be achieved today is very great. Following chapters are devoted to specific popular variations on the theme, but anyone planning to devise a scheme of decoration for a Victorian interior would do well to consider precisely which aspect of the era they find most appealing, and then follow up these general guidelines with more specific study of styles and motifs with the help of some of the original source-books listed in the bibliography. The richness of this archive material, coupled with the probability of finding furniture and other objects of the period at a reasonable price, and the availability of good reproduction papers, fabrics and other elements, make the High Victorian period one of the most interesting in terms of attempting an evocation of an earlier style.

THE AESTHETIC AND ARTS AND CRAFTS MOVEMENTS

1870 · 1890

THE AESTHETIC MOVEMENT was a fashionable name for a fashionable phenomenon. In the 1860s the increasing ugliness and poor design of mass-produced goods led to a reaction in favour of beauty not only in art but in daily life. This reaction began among those most closely involved in design and other matters of aesthetics, namely the artistic community, but spread in the 1870s to a wider public, in the form of smart society. Later still, in the 1890s, it reached the middle-class sitting room. The Arts and Crafts Movement sprang from the same source, but had a wider and more complex influence on art and decoration. Its overriding concern was to maintain and advance the decorative arts, chiefly through the promotion of handcrafted goods. The single most influential figure in both areas was William Morris (1834-96); the Pre-Raphaelite-artist, Utopian socialist and designer of genius.

Morris was a protégé of Dante Gabriel Rossetti, the Pre-Raphaelite painter and poet. He and Edward Burne-Jones carried the Pre-Raphaelite Movement from painting into decoration and design, and in 1861 the practical Morris started a company, Morris and Co., to sell his own and others' work, intending

The Dining Room, Standen, Sussex. Both the house itself and its principal fittings were designed by the Arts and Crafts architect, Philip Webb. The sea-green paintwork of the fitted dressers and buffets was a favourite colour among the adherents of the movement and here forms the natural foil for a fine collection of blue-and-white china. The furniture is a happy mixture of seventeenth-, eighteenth- and nineteenth-century pieces.

to bring good design and fine craftsmanship to the general public. However, the industrialization of all manufacture had by then rendered handmade objects a luxury, so that, just as Morris's socialism remained theoretical, his designs became the preserve of middle-class intellectuals like himself.

Morris and Co. was really the starting point for Aesthetic and Arts and Crafts decoration. The fashion, having begun among artists, owed much to the artistic interests of the day, and in particular to the lifestyle evolved by Rossetti, James McNeil Whistler and other artists living in Chelsea, London. The taste for Oriental objects, blue and white porcelain and Japanese prints had been brought to London from Paris by artists in the late 1850s, while the colours used on walls and woodwork derived from the subtle palette of contemporary art. This decorating style is in fact the first not to be firmly wedded to a particular period of architecture. While some more austere pieces of Arts and Crafts furniture may look well in a timbered or stone-built house of the fifteenth or sixteenth century, almost any room with ordinary chimney piece, windows and doorcase could be decorated in the Aesthetic manner. Morris himself lived in a modern house (Red House, Bexleyheath, Kent), designed by Philip Webb to suit Morris's own furnishings; but moved quite happily with many of the same objects into Kelmscott, a manor house of the sixteenth century (in Oxfordshire) and then into an eighteenth-century town house at Hammersmith. In this respect the Aesthetic taste is the first 'modern' style of decoration, since it relies almost entirely upon colour, pattern and grouping for its effects. The only real anachronism in an Aesthetic interior is bad craftmanship or design. For this reason it would be better to start out with a good Regency chimneypiece than a bad late nineteenth-century example influenced by, but inferior to, the principles of the Aesthetic ideal.

The colour schemes and wallpapers of the Aesthetic taste were generally assembled on the assumption that walls would be treated in the traditional tripar-

Left: 'Summer' by Atkinson Grimshaw (1875). The artist's wife stands in a room in their own house prettily tricked out with the knick-knacks of the aesthetic movement: Japanese fans, blue-and-white ceramics, an Arundel print and an old Chinese teapot. The furniture is eclectic including some Dutch marquetry and there are kelims on the floor. The figured muslin blind casts an aesthetic shade.

Above: The Drawing Room, Kelmscott Manor, Oxfordshire. The old house in which Rossetti lived with Janey and William Morris retains the atmosphere of a temple of Pre-Raphaelitism. This part of the manor is late seventeenth-century, but throughout the house they hung old tapestry and Morris's own fabrics and mixed ancient furniture with Morris and Co. chairs. The result was the ideal aesthetic synthesis.

Elevation of a Drawing room wall by George Aitchison (c.1875). George Aitchison was one of the grandest architectural decorators of the period. This design assumes the use of rare and expensive materials to inlay magnificent polished doors and specially commissioned paintings for the peacock freize gilt decoration. However this last, rich, dark legacy of Pompeii might well be emulated in stencilling or with pictorial frieze-paper.

tite manner. Papers designed by such artists as Walter Crane thus often come in three interrelated but distinct patterns of dado, field and frieze. The frieze may in most cases be omitted, and in such papers was designed to be the dispensable element. The dado rail remains an important part of the room, especially in grander schemes such as those of the architect George Aitchison. Chimneypieces could be of an earlier date without disrupting the scheme. However, as the taste became more popular, overmantels, either painted to co-ordinate with the colour of the walls or ebonized to match the fashionable furniture

designed by E.W. Godwin and others, were introduced. These can still be bought, though good ones are rare and expensive. They should really only be used in conjunction with a compatible chimneypiece and grate in the Aesthetic taste, as they do not look happy on top of an eighteenth-century mantel-shelf.

Doors were, except in houses specially designed by fashionable architects like Philip Webb or Norman Shaw, standard four-panel models. At Linley Sambourne House in Kensington, London, one of the best preserved of Aesthetic interiors, it can be seen how effectively such doors were integrated into a

The Morning Room, Linley Sambourne House, London. *Within an ordinary white-stucco terrace survives this extraordinary time-capsule of the 1870s. The house of a Punch cartoonist is crammed with the densest possible arrangements of furniture and other objects, set against a background of Morris wallpapers and fabrics. Neither the satinwood revival furniture nor the accumulated ornaments are of any great quality; the ensemble is all.*

scheme with decorative paintings on the panels. Mouldings were often picked out in a darker shade of the main woodwork colour, or, if the wood was stained black, in gold leaf. The same treatment was used on the panels of window shutters.

The paintings of Rossetti, Burne-Jones and Whistler give an idea of characteristic colours: the soft olive greens, lustrous grape-purples and hyacinth-blues of Rossetti's drapery, for example, would be an ideal starting point for any room. The deep plum-red or burgundy of old velvet was another favourite colour; and the complementary effects of Whistler's

Nankin blue, watery lemon-yellow and old rose enlarge the Aesthetic palette. White could often be used to striking effect, most significantly in combination with three, four or five other shades from ivory to pale grey. The virtue of Aesthetic colouring lies in its adaptability. From the deeper colours one can assemble a scheme suitable for a dining room or library; while the pale clear shades are ideal in a room intended for daytime use.

Woodwork was very often painted in a flat shade of olive-green, which acted as a foil to the brighter colours of paper and fabrics. Ebonizing, the staining

Above: The Billiard Room, Wightwick Manor, Staffordshire. A shrine to the productions of Morris & Co., Wightwick demonstrates better than any other house how the papers and the textiles when carefully used together create a unique aesthetic. Here the walls are papered with 'Pimpernel', the curtains are in 'Bird', a woven fabric, while the upholstery is 'Tulip and Rose'. The Kidderminster weave rug is 'Tulip and Lily'.

Right: The chimney piece in the Drawing Room, Wightwick. It is impossible to imitate such a grand architectural feature as this, but the use of simple large scale objects grandly arranged is an important element in achieving the look. Fine De Morgan tiles line the fireplace. Note the early brass light fitments above.

and black lacquering of wood, became very fashionable in furniture and woodwork and is found in some of the more ambitious houses of the era. (A similar effect can be achieved with black eggshell paint, finished with a clear varnish.) A complete scheme of ebonized woodwork is eccentric and perhaps overwhelming in a private home, but such a scheme survives in Leighton House, Holland Park, London, built by the artist Lord Leighton in the 1860s, where it makes a striking impact.

The simplest, though not the most economical, way to establish the character of a room in the Aesthetic taste is to use wallpapers of the period. Morris's designs are the most famous historical papers, and approximations to these patterns have been on the market for the last twenty years. However, most commercially produced reprints are not made to scale with the originals, and certainly not in the intended profusion of colours. Morris papers and fabrics were frequently printed with four separate woodblocks, one for each colour, often with supplementary blocks for more elaborate effects. Many reproduction papers are based on fabric designs and are reduced in scale and colour, but it is possible to obtain 'authentic' papers; some seventy-five hand-printed designs, using the same woodblocks and mostly the same colours as the originals are available. Other designs involve having the batches handprinted to your order, and are therefore a great, if desirable, luxury. Almost none of the available fabrics is available in its original form. Most papers and all fabrics which can be bought in the correct colourways are screen-printed and less dense and vibrant in effect than other reproductions. (Samples of original papers and fabrics are collectors' items, and you would need to be lucky or very rich to obtain such rarities.)

Given these limitations, there are still some reasonable solutions to the problem of authenticity. Sparing use of the best of the commercially available Morris facsimiles, in small areas like cushions, adds density of pattern to a room. If these pieces are set against a

The Solar, Great Dixter, Northiam, Sussex. The charms of Great Dixter depend upon the beauty of its timbers. Parts of the house are ancient and the celebrated architect, Sir Edwin Lutyens used beams from other old structures to create extra rooms. The furnishings reflect this fascination with the mellow qualities of old wood and include both handsome rustic pieces such as refectory tables and intricately inlaid marquetry-work cabinets of the early eighteenth-century. Above the original four-centred arch of the chimney textile hangings add another rich note.

plain background of dark wool, cotton or velvet in an appropriate colour, such as a characteristic effect will be achieved. Plain fabrics were often used in conjunction with Morris's and other designers' work. The drawing room at Clouds, in Wiltshire, surely one of the most nobly scaled and yet intensely livable interiors of the period, had plain linen curtains for summer use, with Morris loose covers on chairs and stools. One or two of Walter Crane's wallpaper designs have recently been reproduced accurately in America, though these again are expensive.

Carpets present the same problem: no one except the rich collector will buy an Arts and Crafts carpet of the period; and none is made in replica today. The solution is to look at the colouring of the originals, and also at the practice of contemporaries of Morris who baulked at the price of his products and used Oriental rugs instead. Soft blue, deep red and ivory, or moss-green, gold and brown, are typical Morris colourways, and since these can be found in Oriental rugs, old Persian carpets are in general the best solution to carpeting the Aesthetic interior. For a grander look, old faded rugs should be scattered in a patchwork across bare boards. A more austere effect, according closely with purer Arts and Crafts principles, is to have one good old rug laid over rush matting. Fitted carpeting in Morris patterns is an anachronism.

The last years of the nineteenth century coincided with the first manifestations of modern technology, which included electric lighting. It is still possible to buy original fitments made either by Benson and Co. or by GEC in the last twenty years of the nineteenth century. The proliferation of bright, brassy and cheap reproduction lighting is more of a hindrance than a help to authenticity; old oil lamps and, in particular, early reading lamps with green glass shades come closest to the correct effect. The general feeling in artistic circles was that gas was unaesthetic, and electricity, when it came in, too glaring and unflattering. Oil was the preferred means of lighting, often with silk or metal shades to

A Parlour, Daneway House, Gloucestershire. The simple countryfied taste of the Arts and Crafts designers and furniture makers Ernest Gimson and Sydney Barnsley is here exemplified by their own furnishings set against austerely plain plaster walls. A pierced and hammered candle-sconce and a frame of photographs of old Cotswold houses are the sole enlivening features of this serious statement of an earnest aesthetic.

diffuse the light. Electrified fitments with similar shades can produce much the same effect but with a more acceptable level of illumination. Wall-lights are not typical of the style, until electricity came in, and central lights were chiefly confined to the metal corona, supporting a silk shade, used over the dining-room table.

Though a greater degree of clarity and sparseness of effect is detectable in some prototypical Aesthetic interiors, as for example the Clouds drawing room, such effects are relative. The typical middle-class or bohemian Aesthetic interior is to the modern eye

densely furnished to the point of being cluttered, but in fact a logic governs even the most closely packed sitting room. The fashion for grouping furniture conversationally extended to interiors in this style. Thus the main focus of a room would be the chimneypiece, but subordinate areas of interest might be a piano, easel or group of palms. An artfully contrived casualness of effect was regarded as a desirable and original way of disposing furniture and objects around a room. Pictures and ornaments tended also to be grouped, to emphasize their effect. In artists' studios, which were often publicized in the popular magazines and papers, an easel, half-draped with old velvet, might support a choice sketch from the master's hand, while beside it would stand a plinth supporting a fragment of Greek sculpture, inspiration to the artist, or a fine Oriental vase for a note of colour. Such window dressing, cunningly employed by artists to encourage patrons, found favour also with a wider public in a domestic setting.

It is still possible to buy good Morris and Co. furniture: a Sussex rush-seated sofa need cost no more at auction than a modern upholstered settee; and single chairs and small armchairs are also still available. However, a close look at photographs of the period reveals that it was not typical of these rooms to be furnished only with modern 'designer' pieces. All kinds of English and Continental furniture from the sixteenth to the eighteenth century appear. Obviously some pieces of the 1860s to the 1890s are needed to set the date of the room, but earlier furniture can also be used. Tables were almost always draped with new or old fabric; any kind of small and inexpensive historic textiles will supply a rich background for ornaments. Care needs to be exercised here, for the Aesthetic interior is not characterized by ordinary domestic bric-a-brac. Small bronzes after antique statuary, Oriental ceramics and, in particular, blue and white Chinese export porcelain are examples of the type of decorative object favoured. A hundred years ago the porcelain would have been eighteenth-century; today you might use small pieces from Chinese stores. Beware, though, of trying to make a bold statement with a large-scale modern ginger jar: the more noticeable the object, the more authentic it must

be. Be sure, to paraphrase Oscar Wilde, that your blue and white is worth living up to. A profusion of cut flowers in glass vases or bowls is a timeless but effective means of dressing an Aesthetic room.

Picture-hanging at this time was dense, though not necessarily symmetrical. Though each wall might be dominated by a central canvas, drawing or mirror, the works around it could be hung in a jigsaw puzzle of great complexity. Frames butted close upon each other: narrow black frames for drawings and prints, somtimes with a libe of leaf and for oils one of the typical gilded gesso frames, of which the Watts moulding was the most widely used. Most suppliers of secondhand frames can supply moderate-sized examples on request. Assuming you did not collect nineteenth-century master drawings when they cost a few pounds each, the problem of what to hang on the walls is more easily solved for this period than for most others. Drawings by unknown hands can still be bought inexpensively and make a worthwhile backdrop to a room. Engravings after the great Victorian artists are themselves collected today, but unsigned examples in period frames can still be picked up for the same price as an unmounted drawing by an unknown. Small, heavy frames in black or gold can be fitted with old mirror-glass, and these give the necessary depth to such a picture hang.

In all this, the best way to achieve the feel of early Arts and Crafts taste is to compare your intended scheme with the aesthetic of paintings by Rossetti, Whistler or Burne-Jones. In this period contemporary arts provide not just a documentary source for correct detail, but the very inspiration of the style, and in large degree its *raison d'être*.

The Drawing Room, Clouds, Wiltshire. Philip Webb in his later manner, tending towards the Queen Anne Revival, created in this house what some regard as a near perfect expression of the taste of that influential group of young, intellectual aristocrats who called themselves 'The Souls'. Upon a great Morris carpet chairs are set in conversational groups around tables bearing plain glass vases brimming with simple country flowers. There are shelves for blue-and-white china and bookcases filled with handsomely bound books. Note the extensive use of white.

ART NOUVEAU

1890 · 1901

THE FASHION FOR the style of architecture, painting and the graphic and applied arts to which we give the name Art Nouveau was in historic terms a short-lived one. Emerging in the early 1890s, it peaked at the turn of the century, only to become, in fashionable circles at least, completely *passé* within a decade. Although historians of taste have convincingly revealed many of the origins of the style in the work of English Arts and Crafts designers such as Arthur Heygate MackMurdo, and in spite of the fact that Britain produced a number of the greatest exponents of it, such as Aubrey Beardsley and

Charles Rennie Mackintosh to name only two of the most remarkable, there can be little doubt that Art Nouveau was viewed in its time and for many years subsequently as something of an undesirable foreign intrusion into the well-ordered development of English taste. Of course for some aesthetes and the self-consciously avant-garde the association with decadence constituted some considerable measure of the appeal.

As it developed on the Continent, Art Nouveau took two different paths; one was based on elongated rectilinear forms and tight, precise floral

The Bedroom, Hill House, Helensburgh, Glasgow. Charles Rennie Mackintosh, the Glasgow architect is more than any other British designer associated with art nouveau and the drive to harness the ideals of the Arts and Crafts movement to the emerging challenge of mass-production. The swirling forms of French art nouveau are far removed from the highly disciplined rationale of Mackintosh's all-white bedroom; the first step towards the aesthetic of modernism.

The corridor and staircase at Hill House. While the rooms at Hill House all share a light tonality, Mackintosh here indulges his delight in the graphic use of subdued and brighter colouring. Notice how the small door panels are echoed in the geometric patterns in the wall panels and again in the regular rectangular patterning at the corners of the rug.

ornament; the other was composed of wild, flowing curvilinear elements characterized by a restless 'whiplash' line. The austere elegance of the former derived from the aesthetic of Mackintosh and other designers who became known as the 'Glasgow boys' and became most popular and influential in Germany and Austria. A number of classic Mackintosh pieces such as his distinctive high-backed chairs are available in reproduction, although the complete integrated masterpieces of line and proportioning that survive from his hand are not really susceptible

of imitation. The second, curvilinear strain, on the other hand, found its greatest expression in France and Belgium where architects such as Hector Guimard, the designer of the Paris Metro, and craftsmen such as Emil Gallé pioneered the search for novel and entirely unhistorical forms loosely based on the natural world. In England the artistic minority which espoused the style seems to have drawn inspiration from both strains and, often with reckless abandon, united elements from both.

In England, rooms in the Art-Nouveau taste are in

A window seat, Hill House. The built-in sofa beneath the window is flanked by shelving
which serves also as a pair of sofa tables. Conventional grouping is, however, flouted by
the pierced wooden pylons which form the chief decorative motifs of the window area.
These exaggerated verticals are highly characteristic of Machintosh's style at this date.

some ways reminiscent of the 'greenery-yallery'
phase of Aestheticism. The colours favoured tended
towards dull, off-beat greens such as olive and sage;
mustards and other quirky browns; and the whole
range of lilacs, violets and purples. Eccentric division of the wall into very deep friezes of plasterwork
or, more easily imitated today, rich bands of stencilling, broke deliberately with the patterns of the past.
The most popular motifs for such friezes were
flowers waving on long stems and all sorts of stylized
birds, peacocks in particular. Woodwork was either

in harmonizing dark tones or black, or sometimes
in a rather daring ivory-white which revealed the
profiles of mouldings and the outline of fretted
motifs such as cut-out heart shapes.

A number of excellent designers created richly
patterned textiles for the Art-Nouveau room.
Charles Annesley Voysey was one of the most highly
regarded for his printed and woven furnishing
fabrics, but his work was widely imitated by more
commercially opportunistic designers such as the
Silver Studios. As if in deference to the general

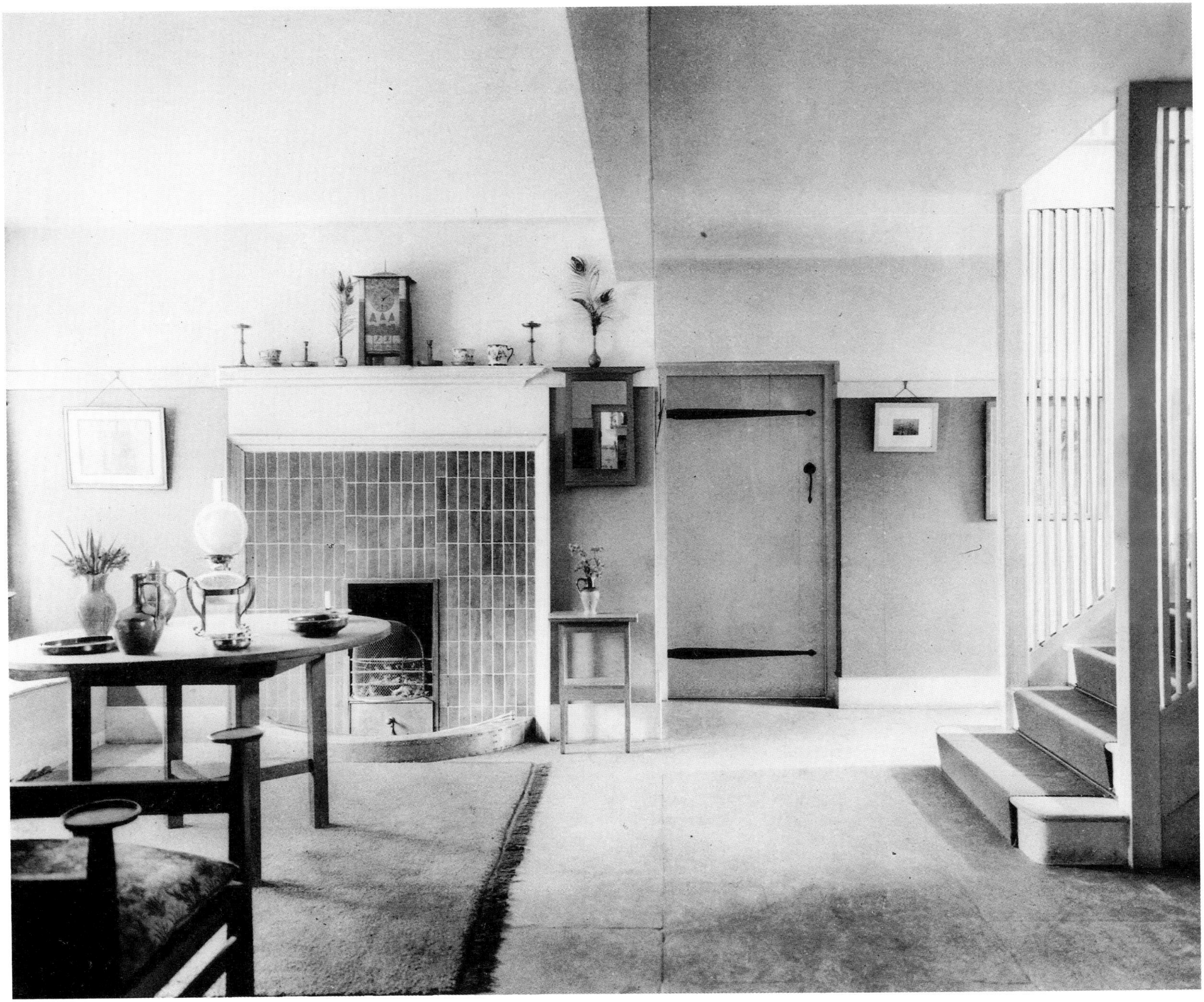

richness of the textiles, curtain treatments were very simple, with straight drapes at the window and, highly characteristically, supported on brass poles over doors as draught excluders. Such effects are not difficult to reproduce, either with old fabrics which you may be lucky enough to find or with modern equivalents. There is not a good range of document fabrics of this period available, but look in department stores and middle-range fabric houses for examples, especially of woven furnishing fabrics, which have the right sort of pattern but which are too pale; these can be dyed to appropriate shades of olive, sage or dull purple.

The best Art-Nouveau furniture was craftsman-made on a one-off basis, but several firms such as Oetzmann's made commercial versions of the extravagantly styled pieces of the day, replete with hammered copper hinges and other fitments. Liberty of Regent St., London, were identified particularly with the promotion of the style, and many of their wares, notably high quality furniture, textiles, ceramics and 'artistic metalwork' can still be found.

Decorative objects of all kinds were arranged in profusion in the Art-Nouveau room, often in preference to pictures. In particular, ceramics of wild outline and finished in brilliant lustres, complicated glasswares and novel light fittings were manufactured in large numbers. Most are now collectors' items, but there are plentiful reproduction light fittings which work well if chosen with care. In general, aim always for an opulence of effect, remembering that during the Art-Nouveau period restraint was derided as an inartistic, middle-class virtue.

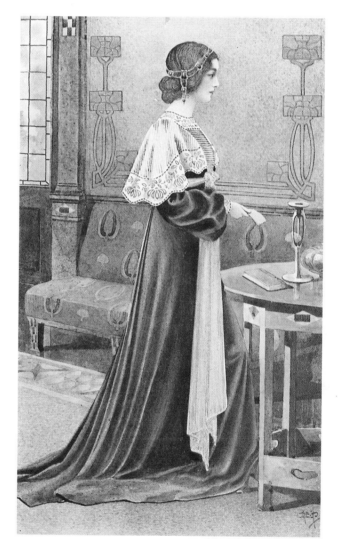

Left: The Hall, The Orchard, Chorleywood, Hertfordshire. This sophisticated essay in a modernistic cottage style by C.F.A. Voysey reveals both the general predeliction of the period for attenuated vertical forms and in Voysey's case a whimsical delight in caricaturing traditional, functional forms such as the strap-hinged country plank door. Here he plays with scale by lining-up the picture rail, doorcase and mantel shelf in an unlikely but successful way.
Above: An art nouveau interior, from **Dress and Decoration,** *a Liberty & Co. catalogue (c.1905). Liberty commercialised the art nouveau style with much success. In this fashion plate can be seen the heart-shaped cut-outs of Voysey and the more lavish stencil decoration inspired by continental art nouveau.*

EDWARDIAN OPULENCE

1901 · 1910

SOME STYLES ARE clearly established in the history of decoration, while others depend as much upon association as on concrete detail for their character. The Edwardian style, with its overtones of luxurious, leisured existence, has become more clearly defined as the expression of an era as that era has grown more distant from the present. The process of revaluation, which occurs first in the literary and visual arts, extends thereafter to the more ephemeral manifestations of an age. Thus, the paintings first of John Singer Sargent, then of William Orpen and John Lavery have become prized, and their critical standing and market value are today correspondingly enhanced.

The novels of the period are as accurate a reflection of the life of the time as the portraits. Henry James, Edith Wharton, and other, less serious practitioners like Elinor Glyn provide a mirror to what has become known as the Gilded Age. The decorative taste of the era comes down to us, like the literature, with a transatlantic inflection, for this is *par excellence* the heyday of the international American set, and of the millionaires who erected on Fifth Avenue in New York some of the most

The Drawing Room, Polesden Lacey, Surrey. Conspicuous consumption here triumphs over good proportion and intelligent use of scale. The brute force of massed gilding cannot entirely conceal the unfortunate outline of the damask panels, nor the crying need for the whole room to be raised upon a dado. However the better pieces of French furniture and the lustre and glitter of expensive finishes demonstrate triumphantly the opulent virtues of the Edwardian style.

extravagant displays in architecture and decoration ever to have functioned as private homes. It follows that Edwardian opulence is, naturally enough, imbued with the atmosphere of great wealth. This may seem a major barrier to recreating the style, but there are elements which are not too hard to copy, and much may be done with large looking-glasses and classical, gilded picture frames.

An important source for the look of the period is *The Decoration of Houses*, a manual of decoration written by Edith Wharton, the American woman of letters, and her architectural collaborator Ogden Codman, who designed for Mrs Wharton the decoration of two of her houses in America. This book was a battlecry against the stylistic vagaries, as they appeared to the authors, of High Victorian house decoration in Britain and North America. Wharton and Codman advocated a return to the architectural principles which had underpinned the *châteaux* and country houses of eighteenth-century France and England. They argued for classical lines against overstuffed upholstery, restrained colours against busy patterns, and for the careful and appropriate planning of a house, instead of the confusions of cosy corners and 'dens'. It should perhaps have followed that the rooms they created were like the stately spaces of Versailles or the more modest splendours of Lord Burlington's Palladian villa at Chiswick, London. In fact, in this, as in every age, its children inevitably stamped their work with a clearly identifiable date: it being next to impossible to escape the spirit of the age. *The Decoration of Houses* makes all the assumptions typical of the Edwardian age: an abundance of cash and servants, and the leisure therefore to live a cultivated and unruffled existence. For this reason their recommendations were taken up chiefly by the professionals who catered to the tastes of people who could well afford to employ an expert to do over their house. Foremost among this new breed of decorators was Elsie de Wolfe, who modified the purist recommendations of the book to allow for practical considerations of daily life in city apartment buildings and other circumscribed urban living spaces, and in the process invented – the word is hardly too strong – the first modern interior-decorating style.

The starting point for Edwardian rooms of this kind is the classical language of architecture. Column and pilaster, dado, frieze and field, and mouldings for cornices of egg-and-dart or other formal motifs give to such rooms a clarity and strength of outline. It is in the proportions of these elements to one another, and in the overall scale of the room, that Edwardian taste often departs from its eighteenth-century French or English model. Ceilings, especially in the new blocks of flats or apartments which had been popularized first in nineteenth-century Paris and New York, were often somewhat lower than before. This is helpful to the modern amateur decorator, for the exact balance which gives an eighteenth-century room its feel is not essential to the Edwardian effect. However, while wall treatments varied according to purse and taste, the wall divisions were always clearly marked. One popular wall treatment

The Blue Drawing Room, Dudley House, London. A small private sitting room in a London palace engulfed by the upholsterer's art. The walls are covered in damask which extends also the lavish folds of the portière *and flows inexorably, like lava, across every surface of the deeply buttoned stuffed furniture. The deepest fringing conceals entirely any structural element of the chairs and sofas. Thus in emulating this style good pieces are by no means a prerequisite of success. Note how the furniture is grouped conversationally into four separate islands of sociability; for this room is intended for smoothly contrived gatherings. The use of prints rather than paintings indicates the room's subsidiary status but might be well worth copying today.*

was the compartmentalization of the wall in panels, using wooden or plaster moulding (run out in commercial quantity), to give something of the atmosphere of Louis XVI *boiseries*. In its most degraded form this sort of decoration was frequently used in large hotels for the reception rooms, where the panels were often filled with wallpaper to resemble stretched fabric, an economy very seldom effective or convincing.

French taste in decoration was highly regarded at this time. In America one encounters great town palaces like that of Henry Clay Frick, now the Frick Museum, Fifth Avenue, New York, where the architects Carrère and Hastings matched point for point the costly materials and noble effect of their French models. Such houses were often fitted out with entire rooms of panelling brought from France, or indeed, in Frick's case, entire rooms lined with canvases painted by Fragonard. A scaled-down version of this impressive form of European shopping might today include the purchase of a modern replica of a Louis XV or XVI chimneypiece, either one of the earlier and more curvaceously scrolled models, or the strictly rectangular variety which stands proud of the wall into the room presenting a broad shelf for the display of porcelain or a clock. These were originally made in stone, and generally still are today. They should be fitted with fire-irons rather than a fixed grate or fire basket, since they were intended to burn wood rather than coal. A more English version of this look would include an Adam-style mantlepiece and a polished

steel or blackleaded cast-iron grate.

The Adam revival of the 1880s which lasted until the early years of this century did not, of course, require the same architectural arrangement of the walls as that of the French style: here a simple dado rail was more appropriate. The colouring also distinguished the English from the French look: there was a move away from patterns in fabrics and wall coverings, and a return to broad areas of simple colour. White and gold with detailing was the preferred colour-scheme in the drawing room and other principal reception rooms. Pale 'Wedgwood' blue was also used, in harmonious combinations with off-white, oyster, lilac and stone-grey. The Adam taste dictated sea-green and apple green, neither of them very close to the eighteenth-century originals. More feminine rooms often came in shades of 'old rose', a dusty pink evocative of the boudoir. Wallpapers may be used, but this is appropriate chiefly in smaller rooms. A 'Regency' stripe, especially if quite broad, is effective, used above a dado rail with either the same or a contrasting colour below, painted solid.

The most marked difference between the originals upon which Edwardian decorators based their style and the resulting decor lies in the arrangement of the furniture. Although Edwardian taste was classical, it was not purged of detail and density of effect. To lay the foundations of an atmosphere of opulence and splendour, it would be good to get a suite of Edwardian Louis XVI-style furniture, a sofa and two or four armchairs, preferably in giltwood and upholstered in silk or satin. The proportions of such pieces

A modern salon, London. This brilliantly successful evocation of the Edwardian grand manner uses a theatrical sense of scale to lend conviction to a simple group of pieces. Applied mouldings hint at carved wood panelling and the sense of height is intensified by the use of lamps placed low on draped tables. The stylish loose covers made of cream damask are gathered in rich folds and secured with sumptuous knots, the fullness of the material complemented by the bagged curtains. The piles of flounced cushions invite a languid feminine repose, but there is a dignity about the room which would accord well with the blue haze of a Havana cigar.

are, like the rooms in which they stood, often out of kilter. Chairs are low, and desks and tables seem slightly clumsy in appearance. Although this style has become more popular and therefore more expensive in recent years, it is still affordable. The grandest pieces are made in imitation of the Boulle of the French court, but French furniture at the other end of the scale, especially nineteenth-century replicas of Louis XVI or Directoire pieces, such as writing desks, jardinières, small bookcases and side tables, can be found, and good plain country furniture can be dressed with silk cushions to give it an urban air.

Chairs, tables and side-tables should be clustered in groups, rather in the late Victorian manner. Armchairs and a sofa around the fireplace are attended by small occasional tables dotted round the room. Books are always kept in freestanding bookcases, and the typical built-in cases flanking a chimney breast will give an English air to a room, as opposed to a purely French revived effect. Palms, though in a way a cliché, have their place in this style of room dressing. A large palm, potted in an imitation *famille-rose* china bowl, and flanked perhaps by attendant smaller flowering plants, captures one richly decorative effect for a reasonable outlay. For authenticity the base of the palm should be bedded in moss or, more extravagantly, wrapped in silk to conceal the rude earth.

The ornaments in such a room are important; and a glance at the illustration of the Countess of Dudley's drawing room, for example, confirms the continuing love of busy tabletops. The English country-house habit of displaying on side-tables and piano lids photographs of illustrious acquaintances, inscribed in more or less endearing terms and mounted in silver photograph frames, dates from these years; and a cluster of black and white portrait photographs, similarly displayed, lends an air to a Steinway: the affectionate inscriptions are of course optional. Add to these some French or oriental porcelain bowls of pot-pourri and perhaps a pretty old porcelain pastel-burner, together with as many small items of silver – other than cutlery – as you wish, and the effect is complete.

The grandest light source is a Baccarat crystal chandelier. Since this is out of the question, any modest cut-glass central fitment will do, if it is big enough. A plain glass chandelier is also appropriate. Since no other ceiling light summons up the right atmosphere of splendour it is probably best to stick to table lamps, which are for the first time absolutely in period. The shades of Edwardian lamps were as intensely furled and draped as the hooped skirts of a French eighteenth-century *marquise*. Pleated silk shades are more accessible and, if you can find them in red or pink silk, will cast an intimate and accurate period glow on the ensemble. Suitable lamp-bases include silver-plated or brass Corinthian columns, and even the classic, modern vase lamp-base is not out of place. However, all lamps should be wired with gold silk 'Art' flex (which is still being manufactured – for suppliers see Lighting, page 202). Modern, white plastic flex simply will not do.

A neatly made and symmetrical picture hang, like that in Canon Valpy's drawing room, may be used on

The Drawing Room, The Close, Winchester by B.O. Corfe (c.1900). This is the drawing room of a conventional, well-to-do clergyman with mildly artistic taste. The fact that the spirit of Adam revival can be detected in these furnishings is perhaps no more than coincidental. The Chinese Chippendale style sofa, satinwood side-tables and carved mirror with sconces are probably good old family pieces rather than modish decorator's additions. However the apple green of the walls and the multitude of gold framed water-colours lend a smart air of lightness and freshness to the room. Only the squat armchairs and sofa indicate the essentially provincial character of this house.

walls which have not been marked out in panels. Where architectural mouldings do define the walls, French eighteenth-century architectural prints hung within the panels create a good sense of order and dignity. Watercolours, drawings and prints are all best framed in slender, gilded mouldings. Since the picture rail is often a feature of the period, the system of hanging prints and paintings on gold wire from brass picture hooks is accurate and can lend, as much as anything else you do, the right sense of place and time.

The Edwardians loved flowers, whether potted or cut, and no arrangement of them can be too lavish in the Edwardian room. Full-blown roses or, in season, great branches of white and mauve lilac, with lilies or any other hothouse flower, are of the age, as are hydrangeas. The keynotes must in every case be luxury and a degree of cultivated artificiality: once more, the novels and portraits of the Edwardian age should be your guide.

A Bathroom, Mount Stuart, Isle of Bute, Scotland. In no department of domestic arrangements were greater advances made in that halcyon period before the Great War, than in bathroom plumbing and fittings. The typical Edwardian bathroom has a bath large enough for aspirant Captain Webbs to practise in and a hot water supply like a tropical geyser. Effective water heating banished forever the agonies of the arctic British bathroom from the new-built mansions of the gilded rich. Such bathrooms were resplendent with tiling, polished marble and varnished mahogany, reminiscent in their technical splendour of the great ocean-going liners of the era. This restored example with its wooden panelling, moulded ceramic border tiles and pendent light-fitments is a splendid evocation of the age of luxury.

ARTISTIC AND IDYLLIC
THE LATER ARTS AND CRAFTS
1910 · 1920

WEALTH AND LEISURE permit the realization of dreams which are otherwise out of the question. The conspicuous magnificence of a revived taste for the French eighteenth century obviously requires the resources of a millionaire, but paradoxically, the dream of the simple life has often proved equally costly. William Morris discovered this paradox and found himself furnishing the houses of an intellectual if not always a financial elite from his Bond Street showroom. The generation of architects and designers who at the end of the century took up Morris's standard were no less idealistic than he, but were rather more worldly-wise.

Foremost of this younger generation was the architect and designer Edwin Lutyens (1869-1944), who has with some justification been compared, in his diversity and brilliance, with that presiding genius of English architecture, Christopher Wren. Lutyens' particular genius lay in his synthesis of the sturdy traditions of the English vernacular with the noblest manifestations of European classicism. Our concern here is not of course with the unapproachable magnificences of Lutyens' 'Wrenaissance' style, but rather with the very livable spaces of his

Kettle's Yard, Cambridge. Jim Ede, who created this house, was one of the leading British collectors of modern art between the wars. His taste embraced the new 'modernism' but his ideals were grounded in the English vernacular tradition and a deep love of nature. White plaster walls, plain linen covers and provincial furniture provide the setting for paintings, sculptures, especially by Gaudier-Breszka, and groups of natural objects such as pebbles and shells.

The Staircase Hall, Munstead Wood, Surrey. In his first major project the architect, Lutyens created for Gertrude Jekyll, the gardener a clever, modern evocation of seventeenth-century vernacular timber building. Bare boards, matting and oriental carpets are the setting for stout country furniture. Thick plain woollen curtains hang straight from rods. An artistic fireplace, with trivet, bellows and pokers, is the perfect place to dry a muddy pair of gardening boots.

smaller domestic projects. In houses such as Munstead Wood, near Godalming, Surrey, his first house (built for Gertrude Jekyll, the great genius of twentieth-century English gardening), he succeeded in combining the simple honesty of a sixteenth-century yeoman's house with the clarity and grace of line of the new era, along with its practical amenities.

The charm of such interiors lies in the happy congruence of varied natural materials and textures: scrubbed or waxed boards and beams, chairs of unpolished wood with rush seats, unbleached linens and plain whitewashed walls. All of this of course is redolent of the countryside, to which so many of the later Arts and Crafts designers felt drawn, but there is also an urban version of the style which employs choice objects and pictures to counterpoint these simpler elements. In this respect the style can be very

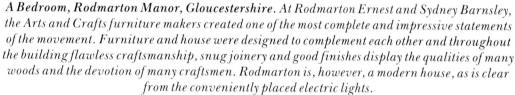

A Bedroom, Rodmarton Manor, Gloucestershire. At Rodmarton Ernest and Sydney Barnsley, the Arts and Crafts furniture makers created one of the most complete and impressive statements of the movement. Furniture and house were designed to complement each other and throughout the building flawless craftsmanship, snug joinery and good finishes display the qualities of many woods and the devotion of many craftsmen. Rodmarton is, however, a modern house, as is clear from the conveniently placed electric lights.

contemporary in its appeal, for it allows beautiful things of diverse origins and dates to work happily together. The intricate patterns of an old Persian carpet or the bolder geometry of a kelim stand out against plain white walls, just as an Oriental vase, not necessarily of any great age, standing alone on a windowsill makes, to some eyes, the most telling note.

A concern for design and a love of simple materials are the keynotes of this aesthetic, and these same basic elements recur through the first three decades of the twentieth century in conjunction with the textiles, carpets and furniture of successive contemporary designers. From Ernest Gimson and the Barnsley brothers working in the Cotswolds at the turn of the century, to Duncan Grant and Vanessa Bell tirelessly decorating Charleston, their eighteenth-century Sussex farmhouse, between the wars, the tradition of simple living and high thinking is an

Oliver Hill's country cottage, Valewood Farm, Hazelmere, Surrey. Oliver Hill was a modernist who liked old things. He brought something of his love of bold scale and dramatic effects even to the furnishing of this weekend cottage, which he shared with the Country Life writer Christopher Hussey. The Zebra skin on the wall and the vast glass bottle standing on the refectory table have a jokey quality which relieves the seriousness of such objects as the seventeenth-century chandelier. Notice that the ceiling beam has been painted white; a 'modernist' touch.

influential strand in the history of English houses.

In its essentials this might seem to be one of the most easily achievable styles in which to decorate. While it must be said that in its deceptive simplicity it offers little cover for the architectural shortcomings of, say, a poorly converted flat in a nineteenth-century house, there are numerous fairly straightforward solutions to the problems you may encounter. It is worse than useless to attempt to fake up the

beams of structural woodwork. Similarly, there is no real substitute for handsome floorboards hewn from oak, and if your floors are cursed with the haphazard consequences of the attentions of a central-heating engineer, then pragmatism dictates that you had better settle for wall-to-wall rush matting. Fortunately this is a stylish and appropriate remedy.

One of the most important things to bear in mind when assembling the elements for this look is the fact

'The White Hall, Howbridge Hall, Witham, Essex' by W.B.E. Ranken (1925). A room in a grand farmhouse, the weekend retreat of the society decorator, Basil Ionides. The panelling has been bleached to avoid the 'magpie' effect which he considered un-chic. Off-whites predominate with pale wood furniture and cream and yellow upholstery and thick whitewash on the walls. Ionides recommended 'Jacobean needlework', that is crewel-work in blue on a white ground, for the curtains in such a scheme.

that all exponents of the Arts and Crafts Movement were in reaction against the vices of mass-production. For this reason it is essential that you review most carefully the existing features of your rooms. It is better not to be too reverent about nineteenth-century speculative builders' taste: those luridly tiled grates of the 1880s, marketed in the vain conviction that the inclusion of a single sunflower motif rendered the whole design 'Aesthetic', were ana-thema to the designers of the Arts and Crafts. If you are lumbered with one of these, but seek the purity of good design, you could remove the grate, sell it and invest the proceeds in a decent pair of seventeenth century English fire-dogs. Such lateral thinking is important when balancing means with ends in the game of creating the new backdrop to your life.

It will be clear by now that this style stands but a step away in many of its essentials from the original

*A window-seat, Charleston Farmhouse, Firle, Sussex. The most famous and most complete
surviving example of a house decorated in the Omega Workshop style. The Bloomsbury painters
Duncan Grant and Vanessa Bell covered every surface of this house with their bright geometric
and stylised floral patterns. Their Anglicised version of Fauvist taste also led them to paint the
furniture and to use jolly hand-blocked or freely-painted textiles.*

scrubbed-pine look upon which so many modern kitchens have been based. Many useful pieces of plain wood furniture, such as cupboards, hanging shelves and blanket chests can still be found which will work in an Arts and Crafts context. Seek well-constructed pieces of good form, and avoid that unpleasant waxy yellow refinishing that mars the beauty of the wood; look, so to speak, for the pale and interesting. Remember also that most good Arts and Crafts furniture is based on sound English vernacular furniture types that have been produced for centuries and are still made today.

The decorative objects in the Arts and Crafts interior tend to be the more beautiful and perhaps older versions of simple everyday objects: old jugs, pewter plates and simple candlesticks mingle with pieces of old Delft or its later imitations. All these will look well arranged along narrow shelves supported with little wooden brackets at the height of the head of the door or above the chimney opening. The solutions to the problems of lighting suggested in the chapter on the Tudor period (see page 21) really derive from those practices which grew up in this kind of interior. Besides the obvious delight and accuracy of candles in beaten metal sconces, practical lighting is most easily provided in the form of wrought-iron lamp-standards and smaller fitments with parchment or vellum shades. Above all, keep everything simple; for this look is one founded in nostalgia for a way of life doomed from the moment that the railways brought the pace and disquiet of modern life to every country town in England.

The Living Room, Charleston Farmhouse. *Light-hearted painted decoration strikes an informal, bohemian note. These artist decorators happily re-covered hideous junk chairs in their loud fabrics and nailed together bookcases from old planks. Paintings hang at random on wires from a picture rail. Country flowers wilting in odd pots created a gloriously haphazard effect which once upon a time culminated in Duncan Grant's Cezanne watercolour drawing-pinned, unframed, to the door.*

METROLAND
SUBURBAN STYLE
1920 · 1930

THE TRAINS THAT killed the English countryside made the suburbs, for they brought semi-rural areas ripe for development within easy reach of the city. The huge expansion of London and the regional cities between the two world wars democratized home ownership and thereby democratized the decoration of houses. For the first time, many ordinary people possessed four or more rooms of which they would one day own the freehold. Building societies were as important as trains, for they now gave the middle classes the necessary funds to buy a house.

The developers who built these suburbs and the people who lived in them both derived their ideal of an Englishman's house from the same sources which had inspired William Morris, Richard Norman Shaw and the later apostles of the Arts and Crafts Movement. If one architect above all others may be credited with the assembly of those architectural motifs and mannerisms which gave rise to the phenomenon of the English 'semi' it is Charles Voysey. Tile-hung upper stories, gables which project over a bay window or descend diagonally to form a porch, and a residual element of timbering on the façade are all features to be found in Voysey's own work, but

A Comfortable Corner in Metroland. This room-set evokes the ideal of domestic bliss marketed so cleverly between the wars by the developers of our English suburbs. Certain elements of this style were all-but universal: dark brown stained woodwork, distempered or all-over patterned papered walls in various shades of porridge and dark polished floorboards. Sub-modernist geometric carpets and strongly coloured moquette or bouclé upholstery struck a livelier note.

which became in the 1920s the staples of suburban speculative builders.

Through front doors laden with strap-hinges and often glazed with a panel of decorative stained glass depicting a galleon in full sail or a sunrise, new owners entered a little world replete with modern conveniences and styled to allow the expression of a measure of individual taste. Scope for original schemes was inevitably bounded by the planning and features of such houses. Everyone knows the standard 'three-up, two-down' layout of these semi-detached homes: on the ground floor there is a front room, or lounge as it came to be called at this date, and behind it a dining-room, smaller because of the stairs and hallway and often linked to the kitchen at the rear by a glazed or double-doored serving hatch; upstairs there are generally three bedrooms of various sizes and one bathroom.

The original fittings of these rooms have, ironically enough, suffered as much from recent attempts at modernization as those in houses of any other period. When built, the reception rooms of all these houses had brick or tiled fireplaces surrounded by a wooden mantel and enclosing a small grate of stove-enamelled cast iron. A picture rail ran round the room at a height of about 8ft (2.5m) where the ceiling height was 9-10ft (2.8-3m). Doors were often panelled in novel arrangements which again owed much to Voysey and his circle; a classic pattern was one in which a large square panel at the top surmounted two or three narrow vertical panels. Door handles are set at chest height and were often of the new lever type, either in bakelite or chromed or bronzed metal. All or some of these elements may have been swept away in an enthusiastic excess of DIY, but all can still be bought today either second-hand or even from the more old-fashioned builders' merchants.

No room of the inter-war years is complete without its full complement of woodwork, all of which should, to be absolutely accurate, be painted or stained and varnished in chocolate-brown gloss finish. Wallpapers were almost universally used in living rooms; and the sample books of the period testify to the extraordinary range of patterns available. 'Porridge' was frequently the ground colour, but this was enlivened with floral and geometric motifs, often in strong and even primary colours. Wallpapers were put up on the field of the wall from skirting board to picture rail; the space above was filled with a co-ordinated frieze paper or merely painted the colour of the ceiling. Borders were an essential accessory, and were not only used to trim the paper immediately below the picture-rail, but were also cut and pasted up to form either panels or decorative corner motifs.

Distemper, the forerunner of modern emulsion paints, was commonly used for all ceilings, sometimes over a textured or patterned paper in which case the frieze was similarly treated. As an alternative to wallpaper, since so many of the patterns of the period will now be unobtainable, walls can be painted in flat colour. This treatment, which was at the time thought to be light and fresh, was often used in bedrooms. The range of colours, unlike that of paints today, was extremely limited, being confined almost entirely to shades of buff, beige and coffee and a few pastel tints such as blues, pinks and that quintessence of the period, *eau-de-nil*.

If the floorboards of the reception rooms were of a reasonable quality, the preferred floor treatment was to lay a patterned square of Axminster or Wilton carpet and to paint or polish the surrounding boards black or dark brown. Otherwise the answer to almost all the flooring problems in the house, from entrance hall via the kitchen to the icy wastes of the English bathroom, was linoleum. By this date lino came in a bewildering range of patterns, chiefly imitating other materials and finishes such as marble, tiling or parquet. Stairs were invariably carpeted with the narrow carpet made for the purpose, either plain or patterned and secured with rods or clips. Upstairs carpets were simpler and usually paler, unpatterned squares being favoured for bedrooms. A distinctive note of period luxury in the grander suburban house

'The Lounge', from the Morrell Countryside Estate prospectus (c.1930). Lattice windows neatly curtained look along the garden path, welcoming the proud new owner to a pastoral brick-lined hearth. Shades of Morris linger over Arts and Craftsy Queen Anne Chairs, while jazz-modern carpet patterns contrast with Mr. Maple's wares. The mirror and the ornaments reflect the cosy style that newly-weds select.

*The Kitchen, 'Baronial Hall', Petts Wood, Kent. The
'Baronial Hall' was one of a number of house models
available in this classic large-scale suburban
development. The technology of this kitchen is little
changed from that of its nineteenth-century counterparts.
There is a Butler's sink, now with a tiled splash-back, but
with surface-plumbed taps unchanged from the turn of
the century. Water was heated by the coke-burning boiler
next to the gas stove.*

ornaments and pictures perjoratively designated by the young housewife of the 1920s as 'clutter'. Thus in the sitting room you would find a three-piece suite of sofa and two armchairs, perhaps a gramophone cabinet in walnut veneer, a folding tea-table and not much else. What animates a room in this style? You may choose from a wide variety of seating types, from the reproduction 'Queen Anne' fireside wing armchair to the fully upholstered elephantine forms of the 'modernistic' designers. Suites were upholstered in moquette cloth or velour which came in either flat colours such as moss green or claret or in the sharp colours and exaggerated geometrical patterns which went by the name of 'jazz modern'. As an alternative, loose-covers in floral-patterned chintz or cretonne were popular. These were often put on for summer and removed in winter, thereby echoing the alternation of thin summer curtains with thicker, draught-excluding winter drapes. Curtains were always straight and hung from flat pelmets of the same fabric, although in bedrooms simple rufflettes were employed to hide the curtain rail.

Dining rooms were similarly regulated by the suite of furniture. This might be in any style but the most characteristic was the 'mock-Tudor' in fumed or dark oak finish. Practical draw-leaf dining tables and heavy sideboards gave a feeling of olde-worlde solidity which was underlined by the use of crimson textiles and often led on to whimsical indulgences of taste such as horse brasses and lampshades made from old legal parchments trimmed with crimson gimp.

Bedroom suites, comprising double or chastely paired single beds, wardrobes and a dressing-table with stool were also available in a wide variety of modern or period pastiche styles. Of these the most distinctive was a bastard version of the Queen Anne style in which the heavy carcases of walnut veneer conspire to compress tiny cabriole legs. In the bedroom the bed would be dressed for the day with a plump satin counterpane and valance and perhaps a lavishly quilted eiderdown, which brought to the

might be a cut-pile Chinese carpet in old rose or deep blue. A hearth rug of this kind would be an accurate addition to a more modest bedroom.

In furnishings this is, above all, the age of the suite. Ideas of house furnishing were to some extent dictated by the relative paucity of domestic help, and so the ideal modern home contained a modest number of useful pieces of furniture and was increasingly devoid of the dense accumulation of

The Tudor Hall, 'Baronial Hall', Petts Wood. The real oak panelling here lends a veneer of respectability to this cramped reminiscence of the Arts and Crafts staircase hall. Other survivors of aesthetic taste include a rather small electric lantern on a chain and a plate shelf above the panelling. The cuckoo-clock, a characteristic feature, recalls perhaps merry holidays in the Tyrol in those innocent days before the rise of fascism.

boudoirs of Harrow-on-the-Hill a little touch of Beverley Hills glamour.

You do not need many framed pictures in such interiors. A watercolour of the harbour at St Ives or an etching of the donkeys at Clovelly would perhaps be a happy reminder of seaside holidays undertaken on the Cornish Riviera Express. Otherwise, mirrors are more characteristic of the age, often oval or segmental in shape, unframed and hung from chains.

When you have achieved the domestic bliss of your perfect suburban interior, one final definitive note at the end of your crazy-paving path should be a wooden garden gate reproducing in its design the rays of the sun setting behind the closing titles of a Hollywood fantasy.

NEO-BAROQUE

1920 · 1930

THE GAMES PEOPLE choose to play, whether in entertainment, literature or decoration, are invariably expressive of more serious underlying needs and aspirations. In the age of the Bullnose Morris and the celluloid collar, cinema-goers thrilled to the Hispanic extravaganzas of Douglas Fairbanks in their desire to escape from mundane suburban realities. Though apparently far removed from such simple pleasures, Virginia Woolf's witty and self-consciously provocative novel *Orlando* (1928), with its loving evocation of the baroque architectural splendours of Knole in Kent, seat of the Sackville-West family, is also an exercise in the same kind of romantic escapism, but for the super-sophisticates of literary and artistic London.

Similar motives encouraged collectors and decorators to ransack the attics of once-grand English houses and the antique shops of Italy and Spain for old brocades, embossed leather screens, vast ecclesiastical candlesticks and Venetian glass chandeliers. The essence of this style lies in a sense of grand scale and an absence of clutter. Even in the smallest room, neo-Baroque decoration should depend for its effects upon one or two magnificent gestures: an

Francis Stonor's bedroom, Stonor Park, Oxfordshire. The fantastical marine grotto of a Catholic bachelor with artistic taste, this room has as its centrepiece a mad bed in the form of a great sea-shell cast adrift in a carved and gilded wooden sea. The neo-baroque look depends upon finding such extravagant objects as shell-grotto chairs, vase fire-baskets and evocatively gloomy pictures. Such effects only work when they are bold and theatrical.

over-scaled architectural column supporting a bust of a seventeenth-century cardinal, or a monstrously periwigged grandee, for example, or perhaps a vast sweep of scarlet brocaded silk borne aloft by carved cherubs clinging perilously to golden ropes and tassels. Such an ensemble, set off by a boldly geometrical floor – either painted or laid out in black and white tiles – need not cost the earth; though the effect, once achieved, may convince your friends that you have inherited it.

Wall treatments should be extreme; either choose the darkest and richest of colours, perhaps in shot silk or taffeta, or, if the space lends itself, aim for the austere nobility of whitewashed walls in the Spanish manner. Against such a background, a few big pieces of furniture will make an impact even if they are outrageously bogus and coarsely detailed. Fortunately, the mania for seventeenth-century furnishings in the 1920s encouraged the makers of reproduction furniture to create a huge variety of practical pieces styled in this theatrical vein. The classic element for the neo-Baroque drawing room is a 'Knole sofa' upholstered in rich fabric and trimmed with yet more rope and tassels. For the dining room, a table might be made from two baroque stone plinths supporting a single massive slab of plate glass. Equally, any largish table will, if dressed with a lavish quantity of heavily fringed brocade or damask, complement some of the many varieties of high-backed, seventeenth-century style chairs. These should have squab cushions, again lavishly fringed and tied on with tassels.

Dramatic lighting is essential to such interiors, and while the great guttering waxen candle might seem to be the most accurately theatrical source of illumination, a number of electric light fittings are equally appropriate for the neo-Baroque room-set. Made in large numbers during the 1920s, and still to be found, are standard lamps, either in 'Spanish' wrought iron or, more amusingly, in wood covered in padded velvet edged in rows of brass nails. These should have shades made of parchment

Osbert Sitwell's dining room, Carlyle Square, London. The best known exponent of the neo-baroque style, both in his prose and his lifestyle, Osbert Sitwell created rooms in his London terrace house which combined the frivolities of the old decorators of Venice with the avant-garde productions of his young artist friends. Notice the shell grotto chairs and other pieces of gilded furniture and the walls upon which a lamé fabric has been stretched.

'Curzon Street Baroque' by Osbert Lancaster (1939). This is one of the series of clever drawings in which Osbert Lancaster anatomised the vagaries of style from the standpoint of the late 1930s. He first named this chic style, a smart decorator's version of the taste of people like the Sitwells and Lady Sackville. Notice the Spanish style ironwork, vast candlesticks and that most characteristic neo-baroque piece, a 'Knole' sofa.

or lacquered card. Central light fittings that will work in this context also abound. All sorts of carved wooden chandeliers in polished, painted, gilded and especially silvered finishes can be employed, and will be enhanced by a sleeve of silk or velvet gathered at regular intervals down the chain. Best of all, however, is the full-blown splendour of a Venetian glass chandelier.

In the absence of oil paintings of suitable scale you can use, in conjunction with more modern furnishing fabrics, large decorative panels of old textiles: colourful embroidery or fragments of tapestry are visually intriguing, but lengths of figured silk such as old altar-frontals, and ecclesiastical vestments, capture precisely that sense of well-worn magnificence so prized by the decorators of the day.

VOGUE REGENCY

1920 · 1930

THIS STYLE, WHICH is not so much a style as a decorative game, was first named by Osbert Lancaster and John Betjeman in *Homes Sweet Homes* (1947), Lancaster's book of architectural cartoons, so light in touch yet to serious in underlying intent. It describes a form of Regency revival, based on the scholarly collecting of enthusiasts such as Edward Knoblock and Lord Gerald Wellesley, but glamourized by the worlds of the theatre and *haute couture* and popularized by fashionable decorators. Its heyday was in the late 1920s and the 1930s, but since the War and, indeed, to this day it has continued to attract camp followers. Anyone seeking a feel of the style in its purest forms need only look to the dust-jackets of Georgette Heyer's novels or the illustrations on a tin of *Quality Street*.

Vogue Regency is a debonair style that obeys no rules, and the more the effect resembles a stage-set, the more completely will it capture that elusive essence of inter-war chic. It is a stripped-down style; it requires few, but boldly stated, architectural features and can as well be done with plaster casts and boudoir bric-a-brac as with real antiques. A room of almost any period which has a ceiling of decent

Angus McBean's bedroom, Endell Street, London. The fashionable photographer, Angus McBean took a house in London's theatreland just after the second World War and transformed it with his inimitable blend of historical accuracy and unbridled frivolity into a tiny Covent Garden version of Malmaison. The lit-en-bateau *is a classic piece, here given appropriately lavish drapery in red contrasting against the theatrical blue sky painted in* trompe l'oeil.

A Vogue-Regency sitting room by Syrie Maugham.
Clean lines, and fitted furniture lend a distinct
character of modernity to Mrs Maugham's version of
the Vogue regency style. Sofa and fitted shelves stand
on an asymmetrical plinth which is, like the rest of the
room, close carpeted. A starred satin pulls together the
lean curtains and self-consciously large pouffe. Only
the bobble-fringe of the pelmets softens the lines of this
room and the spoon-back chair of about 1810 contrasts
strikingly with the modern fitted electric fire.

height lends itself to this treatment. This is the true
preserve of the Regency stripe, which lends added
height and elegance to the proportions, while
strong, clear colours such as lilac or acid yellow and
panels of unframed mirror-glass emphasise the
modernity of the look.

The treatment of the chimney-piece should also
emphasize this modernity. One of plain marble or
marble-painted is best and will be complemented by
the insertion of a *trompe-l'oeil* chimney-board as the
back-drop to a small pre-war electric fire, the most
amusing of which come in the style of Adam grates
or with their enamelled metal casings in a *faux-
marbre* finish. Limit the garniture of the chimney-
piece to just three well-chosen objects: perhaps a
pair of lustres, classically inspired vases or something
suggestive of the Napoleonic period.

Curtain treatments should be dramatic, almost
parodying the colourful asymmetric arrangements
of the Regency. Use silks and especially shiny satins,
in oyster, powder blue or sharp greens, with plenty of
rope and tassels. An abundance of scatter cushions,
also well hung with tassels, should pick up the colours
of curtains and covers, and real afficionados of the
style will complete their fireside ensemble with an
exotically draped pouffe.

There can be no formal plan to the furnishing
of such rooms, for they reflect the *laissez-faire* of the
Jazz Age and the Cocktail Hour. Contrary to the
historical development of room arrangements
whereby furniture came forward from the walls for
social use, the Vogue Regency room is definitively
one in which it is pushed back for partying, revealing the characteristic acres of plain carpet, enlivened
perhaps by a Portuguese needlepoint rug. An elegant Regency sofa or day-bed would strike the right
note, but an upholstered divan might well provide
an effective and economical alternative. Modern
replica side-chairs in the Regency manner can be
grouped with occasional tables such as those amusing examples made to resemble a military drum.
Above all, keep the furnishings light in form and

Left: The Library, 5, Belgrave Square, London. Dolly Mann, the decorator who put Regency into vogue created for the millionaire socialite and politician, Sir Henry "Chips" Channon this chic library for entertaining. The bookcases have Napoleonic crossed spear motifs whilst above are panels painted as trompe l'oeil *bas-reliefs. The small period sofa in striped satin is a conversation piece, while the big modern white sofas are better adapted for the serious exchange of political and social intelligence.*

Right: The Map Room, Port Lympne, Kent. Philip Sassoon, politician, aesthete and amateur aviator, commissioned the smart architect Philip Tilden to create in his extravagent new country house an architectural space worthy of decoration by the greatest muralist of this century, Rex Whistler. The elegant arabesque profile of the barrel vault was designed to complement the trompe l'oeil *striped tenting. The rest is Whistler's genius.*

character, perhaps enlivening some duller pieces with a few judiciously applied gilt-brass stars or anthemion ornaments taken from an architectural brass founder.

Vase or pillar table-lamps with simple shades of card, parchment or silk are correct, but a number of the available wall-bracket fittings in versions of the French Empire style are appropriate for the Vogue Regency room; one of the most stylish of these is based on old candle-sconces supported on crossed arrows. These again reflect the popularity of military themes, and might well be made the starting point for a collection of pictures and prints such as coloured engravings of the uniforms of some of the more glamorous hussar regiments, framed in *passepartout* ovals.

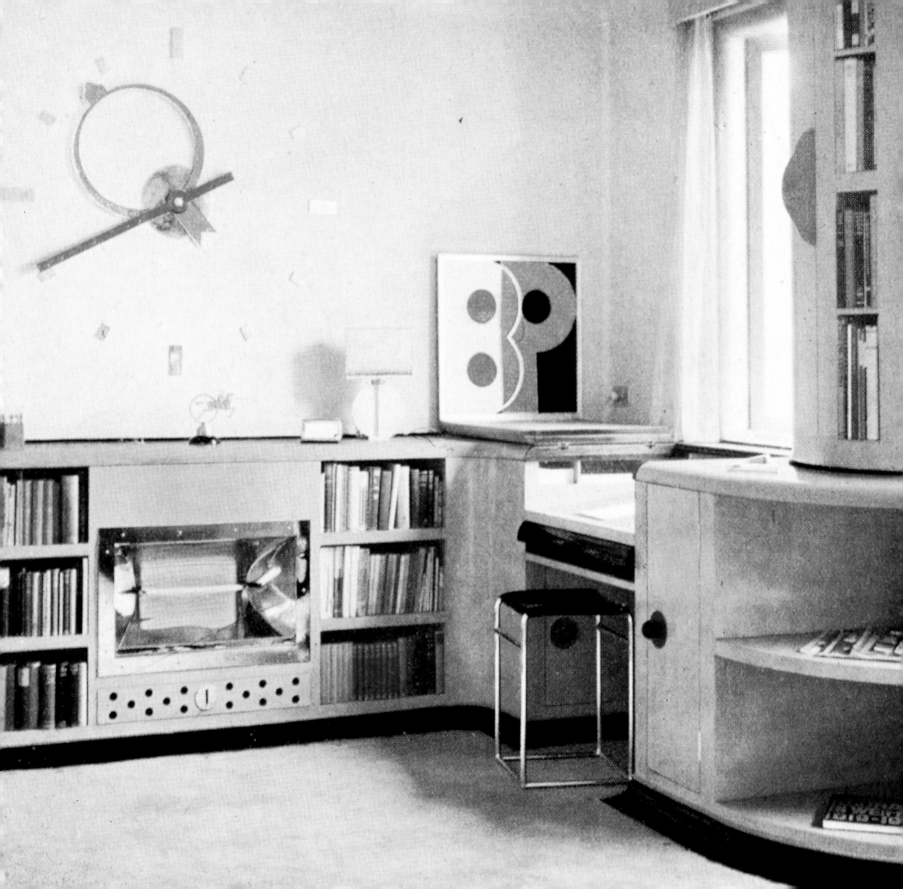

ART DECO

1925 · 1935

T HE NAME ART DECO, so indiscriminately used, has in fact a precise origin. It was coined from the title of the vastly influential *Exposition des Arts Décoratifs*, staged in Paris in 1925. There, in the pavilions of what must be accounted one of the most remarkable manifestations of the arts of furnishing and decoration ever assembled, those Continental traditions of high finish and rich surface ornament confronted for the first time the radical, reductivist aesthetic of the Modern Movement. The results were new types of furniture, textiles, ceramics and metal-work; and these elements were assembled in interiors of strikingly imaginative, if perhaps not always wholly successful, eclectic daring. Measured against the touchstone of French excellence, the pavilions of the other participating nations cut a sorry figure, and for this reason the best of English decoration in this manner bore a heavy French accent, while home-grown versions consciously aimed to make up in cosy domesticity for what they lacked in Continental chic.

As a style dependent above all else upon colour and pattern, Art Deco worked very well whether it was imposed upon existing or newly built rooms. The seeming simplicity of the style was for many 1920s'

Ashley Havinden's study, High Point, North London. As a decorative style 'Modernism' can have both wit and originality; in the hands of the designer Ashley Havinden it had both. The residual cornice and the great big Toy-Town clock are clever enhancements of the seriously thought out built-in furniture. Note those most characteristic conveniences of inter-war comfort, the fitted carpet and the chrome wall-mounted electric fire.

A roomset by Betty Joel. *Betty Joel's work was typical of the more colourful aspect of design in the period between the wars. In this set she showed against a back-drop of Canadian pine veneer, in the manner of the French decorator Jean-Michel Frank, a collection of her bright, geometric pieces. The sofa, ziggurat bookcases and the brocade-covered cube chair all reveal an unmistakable debt to the work shown at the Paris* Exposition des Arts Décoratif *of 1925.*

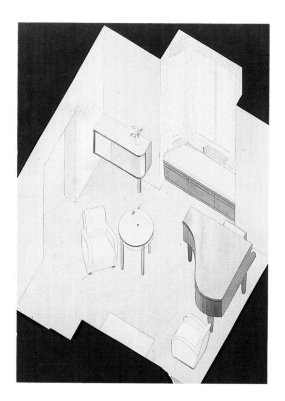

Axonometric design for a room by Gordon Russell Ltd. (1935). *This design, drawn as if seen from above, aims for something of the same sense of drama as film-directors sought when they shot massed chorus-girls from vertiginous angles. By thirties standards the room is quite densely furnished with fat armchairs and a baby-grand piano, but the sense of space is enhanced by the use of plain carpet and built-in furniture in pale woods.*

home-makers a trap: it was all too often assumed that, by hanging some bright geometric or floral French fabric at the windows and scattering a few ill-considered cushions on the drab expanses of English upholstery, the effect would, as if by magic, create a *salon*. Any serious attempt to recreate this look must take due account of the underlying decorative principles that dictated a unity of effect and an emphasis on quality.

Since few architectural elements are vital, you should concentrate to begin with upon the meticu-

lous preparation of all the surfaces of the room. Clean lines and smooth planes are essential to the brilliantly reflective, lacquered or glazed surfaces of the Art Deco room. Establish a dramatic scheme composed of contrasting colours for walls and woodwork. Characteristic wall colours included ultramarine and other deep blues, lilac, all manner of reds from crimson to burnt orange, and rich dark greens. Even glossy black enjoyed a vogue. Against the reds, lacquered black or dark green were used; black was also used with lilac; while the blues lent themselves to red woodwork or, more subtly, other shades of blue. Black as a wall colour required either red or silver as its complement. Both gold and silver leaf, usually applied with the individual leaves showing as squares or toned and splattered, were popular if expensive. These effects can be achieved today, but must be done very well or not at all. One simple economy is to employ the traditional substitutes, Dutch Metal (brass leaf) for gold and aluminium for silver, both of which give a close approximation to the effects of the precious metals. (These must be protected from discoloration by varnish.)

Without considerable luck you must expect to spend a good deal of time, and perhaps money too, in search of original textiles in the Deco style. There are very few authentic patterns in furnishing materials available, and so the skill and, indeed, the fun of the game lies in spotting those modern textiles which combine geometric and bold floral motifs with colours verging on the garish that are more likely to be found on market stalls selling dress fabrics than in the better fabric-houses. Such stuffs as printed satins and gold and silver artificial fabrics will, if sufficiently well made-up with heavy interlinings and good-quality trimmings, carry the theatrical effect. Large carpets are equally hard to find, especially in good condition, and here the solution may be to lay a square of plain carpet in a bright and characteristic colour against floorboards finished in glossy black or even another colour. If you have the good fortune to find a hearth rug of the period, it could be a starting point for a colour scheme and a finishing touch for the room.

The finest pieces of furniture in the Deco style, for the most part French, are now collectors' items and therefore command the same kind of prices as good-quality antiques. These fabulous pieces in rare woods and exotic materials such as ivory and sharkskin were, to the chagrin of the best designers, much imitated in more common materials. It is these, at best, that you may hope to find, but they will at least give you the right types and basic outlines to furnish a room. Characteristic of the drawing rooms of the day were plump upholstered sofas and armchairs, often slip-covered in shiny fabrics, piped at the edges, and outrageous pastiches of the more opulent period styles, such as asymmetrical Napoleonic sofas. Little pairs of two-tiered tables with glass shelves supported by brass, acorn-finialed legs flanked sofas or nestled by the fire in order to keep close at hand those necessities of 1920s' life, the white telephone, the cigarette box and the silver ash-tray. Drawing-room lighting, as in other parts of the house, became much more subtle and complex, with many new forms such as standing and wall-mounted uplighters. The former generally stood in a corner or, in an arrangement where the sofa stood in front of the window, were placed so as to light up the curtains at night. More conventional table-lamps were made from Oriental vases on carved cherry-wood stands; they invariably had panelled or pagoda-shaped silk shades, as heavily fringed as the forehead of the 'vamp'. Other forms of table-lamp included glass columns, plain or painted turned wooden balusters and a wide variety of the new purpose-made bases in various forms and of many different materials.

In the bedroom a veneered suite of divan with headboard, wardrobes and dressing-table might well display the species of agitated ornament to which we give that telling name 'Jazz-Modern'. The bed itself, to be in the height of fashion, would have reflected what high-street furnishers knew of the luxury boudoirs of the stars of stage and screen. But where furniture designers' fantasy really took flight was in the creation of a new and chic Chinoiserie, a taste reflected in the contemporary vogue for that most decorative game, Mah-jongh. In this rerun of the perennial favourite among the exotic styles, ordinary domestic furniture was suddenly paraded in black, scarlet or pale yellow japanning. The treatment was given even to standard-lamps and firescreens, the latter being enriched with mandarins, pagodas and fiery dragons.

My new living-room

'My new Living Room' from I Decorate My Home by Derek Patmore (1936). *A scheme in the quintessential Art Deco colours, pale green and cream. Fat moquette upholstered chairs with the useful flat arms of the period, stand on a carpet with a large scale Greek key border. There are long, low bookshelves in a unit which also houses the chrome inset electric fire. The curtains are made from a rough weave linen block-printed with a bold pattern.*

INTERNATIONAL MODERNE

1930 · 1939

RATIONAL DESIGN and the desire to reduce the home to merely 'a machine for living in', in the words of Le Corbusier, have always been the cherished preserve of those architectural theorists, planners and others who delight to meddle as 'experts' in the affairs of the public. Modernism in all its philosophical manifestations in Europe between the wars sought to hustle the unsuspecting masses into a brave new world, which rapidly proved to be as much a fantasy as the self-conscious ruralism of the Arts and Crafts Movement. It was in Germany, prior to the rise of Nazism, that the group of designers which formed around Walter Gropius at the state design school, the *Bauhaus* in Dessau, set out to restructure in every essential the familiar modes of European domesticity. These messianic engineers of modern life stripped walls of their mouldings and furnishings of every superfluous detail in the desire to reduce all to the cleanliness and efficiency, as they saw it, of the hospital or laboratory.

Scattered to the four winds of Western democracy by the totalitarian Nazi state, Gropius and his followers carried the new aesthetic to nations which remained perhaps unconvinced of the value of the

The Drawing Room, Syrie Maugham's Kings Road house, London. Mrs Maugham designed the 'all-white room' for her own house in 1929-30 and it became the most celebrated scheme of its day. It combined a superficial gloss of modernism with a good deal of comfort, the low sofas and deep sculptured-pile carpet adding a note of luxury. The other furniture was in pale and pickled woods contrasting with the chic chrome mirrored screens.

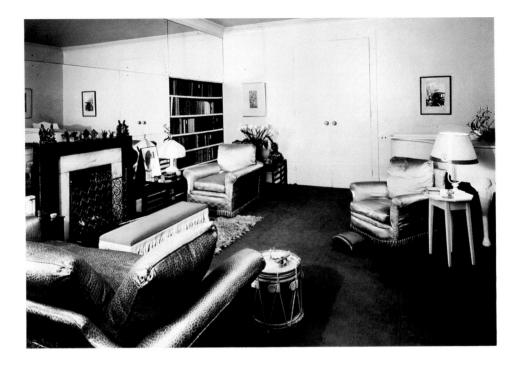

*Gertrude Lawrence's drawing room, Portland Place, London. This plain room
decorated by Ronald Fleming for Gertie Lawrence displays more dash than cash. The
wall of mirror and the satin-covered chairs could be the set for a Noel Coward play.
Note the Vogue Regency touches in the drum table and the lyre-base of the table-lamp.*

grand social design, but fell with delight upon the chic sophistication of clean lines and a daring use of new materials such as chrome and glass. Smart society had already been introduced to the look mainly in terms of its appearance as a style appropriate to public spaces such as the foyers of theatres and cinemas and the cocktail lounges of the grander international hotels. But as early as 1929 the publication of the first photographs of a room decorated by Syrie Maugham in her house in Chelsea, London, created considerable excitement for the way in which it showed how *Moderne* style could be used in smart and comfortable drawing rooms. Syrie's 'all-white room', as it came to be known from its subtle use of pale paintwork, off-white, loose-weave textiles and bleached-wood furniture, set a fashion which has, in a sense, lasted ever since.

There is no better model to follow than this if you wish to recreate the cool urbanity of 1930s' style. Its essence is the emphasis on horizontality, and so it will work best in a room in a house or block of flats of the period where every element has that streamlined quality associated in the popular imagination with the great ocean liners of the inter-war years. In such apartments this emphasis will be felt particularly in the form of the windows, in which both the overall shape and the individual panes will echo the horizontal theme. For this reason the look will

Thirties' technology in the kitchen. This exhibition set is based on the typical city basement kitchen of the nineteenth century. What makes it fresh is the range of new fitted cupboards which incorporates a sink unit. Older elements such as the table and traditional Windsor chairs have been painted to match the cheerful check curtains.

seldom work in older houses where everything is built to a vertical aesthetic and where surviving architectural details would have to be removed. It may, however, very well add spice and elegance to those bland interiors of the 1950s and 1960s, built in what passed for an International *Moderne* style, but which are all too often impoverished of detail and devoid even of the charms of the original.

As if in complete reaction to the vivid colouring first popularized by the visits of Diaghilev's *Ballets Russes* and taken up with enthusiasm by the designers of the Jazz-Modern age, the tonalities of the 1930s were subtle and usually pale. All-white rooms were never stark white, but depended upon the careful use of shades from ivory white through to pale creams, champagne and even dove grey. In rooms with a single colour theme the orchestration of different tones provides the variations necessary in order to avoid monotony. The colours favoured were still governed, at least for the majority, by the limitations of the paints commercially available; thus in city penthouses as in suburban villas, *eau-de-nil*, pale blues and 'Germolene pink' were almost universally employed.

Textile design in this period enjoyed a surge of creative activity, most notably in the work of designers such as Marion Dorn and painters who turned their hands to the applied arts such as Paul Nash and

Left: A Morning Room by John Hill. A grand eighteenth-century room updated to thirties modern classicism. The original features are respected and everything is painted white. This high key is followed through in thin white fish-tailed pelmets and curtains of the same fabric stencilled with a stylised feather motif in blue. The rug is the most modern element whilst the furniture is a mixture of old and new.

Above: A Thirties Room in Beige. This roomset, originally created as an advertisement for wallpaper, shows a number of the smarter features of thirties style adapted with only varying degrees of success to the constraints of the average small, suburban living room. Notice in particular how the long, low lines of the furnishings and the horizontal emphasis of the wallpaper pattern, which work well in larger, open-planned spaces of the period, create a ludicrous effect here. This room is a warning.

McKnight Kauffer. The fabrics and carpets designed by these and other famous names are now much collected, but you may be able to find examples of their commercially produced ranges, which included for instance a number of useful rugs and carpets by Dorn. In curtain and upholstery fabrics there are many printed patterns which evoke the period, but for upholstery and also for curtains the 1930s' style loose-weave and plain-textured materials that are still manufactured and widely available today will give an excellent effect. Good-quality parquet flooring was often to be found, even in speculative developments of houses and flats, and surprising as it may seem you would be true to the taste of the day were you to lay over such a polished wood floor an off-white carpet with a 'sculptured' or 'shag' pile.

No set of a Noel Coward play would be complete without a white boudoir-grand piano and a magnificently appointed cocktail cabinet. Either might prove the perfect starting point for an evocative arrangement of 1930s' pieces. Realistically, since both are expensive items, there are plenty of more modest pieces still to be found – even in second-hand furniture shops – which will set the scene: long, low sofas, perhaps with tubular chromium frames, glass and chrome drinks tables and trolleys; and dwarf bookcases and chests of drawers in limed or pickled oak and other woods. Fortunately for those attempting to assemble enough practical pieces of furniture to do their rooms in the International *Moderne* manner, most of the classic designer pieces such as Marcel Breuer's famous tubular chair and Mies van der Rohe's 'Barcelona' chair are now reproduced. Though not cheap they have the advantage of being, unlike many fakes and 'repro' pieces, made to the exact original specifications.

Syrie Maugham had a way with old paintings. She painted the frame white and, throwing away the canvas, inserted a piece of looking-glass. This funny and true story points up an important aspect of the look: pictures really are superfluous here. Pick your ornamental objects carefully and use them sparingly. An old bakelite telephone in black or, better still, ivory, is one of the best accessories of the period. It must have a woven-silk covered cord. A cocktail shaker is a practical asset, but its place is inside the cocktail cabinet. Table-lamps are among the few utilitarian objects which may authentically adorn the room. Several different types are possible: columns of glass, chrome or alabaster; vases in white or celadon eggshell-crackle glaze; and all manner of cunning desk-lamps incorporating penholders or ashtrays. Thus equipped for cocktails and laughter, you may embark upon your private lives.

The Lounge, 42, Upper Brook Street, London. This large room is in a development of apartments in a modern block. The designer of the room was Serge Chermayeff, a pioneer of the modern movement who formed a partnership with the Bauhaus architect Mendelsohn. This interior is marked by the horizontality of all its elements and in particular by the precise ordering of the built-in fitments. There is a kind of residual chimney-piece, with a chrome electric fire and a 'chimney garniture' of two old wine bottles. The beige day-bed and other pieces of laminated wood furniture are typical avant-garde pieces and the light fittings, which include a wall-mounted angle-poise lamp, reflect the very latest developments in home technology.

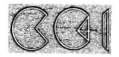

WARTIME

1939 · 1945

IT IS A FALLACY to suppose that all decorating in Britain ceased with the declaration of hostilities, just as it is mistaken to assume that the social milieu in which high decorative style had flourished in the 1930s was immediately dispersed as its chief protagonists became absorbed with preoccupations of war. A reading of the memoirs and diaries of Nancy Mitford, Chips Channon or, most appositely, James Lees-Milne will readily reveal the extent to which many aspects of ordinary daily life continued. Decorators who were at work on schemes carried on with them. It was only gradually, as people were called away for more serious work and as a scarcity of materials began to make it difficult to carry out projects, that such work tailed off.

There were in a sense two reactions to these wartime exigencies, one unofficial and localized, the other nationally organized and directed. The ingenuity of individuals resulted in many inventive and often hilarious solutions, such as the elaborate swagged curtains confected by the brilliant decorator John Fowler using dyed army blankets and oddments of *passementerie*.

At the other extreme, the Government responded

An embattled dining room in 1940. While some sat out the Blitz at the Ritz, life was throughout the second World War, for the majority, more literally a matter of bare survival. Few who lived through it had any desire after 1945 to preserve nostalgically the domestic evidence of those years of deprivation. This roomset therefore comes as close as anything can to evoking something of the feel of the period.

The living room of a 'Pre-Fab'. Pre-Fabricated housing was the National Government's solution to the problem of re-housing thousands of bombed-out families. Many of these had lost everything and so needed not only roofs over their heads but cheap basic furniture. The 'Utility' scheme aimed to provide this and designers who had previously wrestled with form and function only on a philosophical level now found themselves confronted by the reality of human need.

to the twin problems of shortages and the need to make available, as cheaply as possible to bombed-out families, basic furniture and other necessities, by establishing design teams and manufacturing groups to husband diminishing resources and to set minimum standards for the production of decent household goods. Few people will wish to set up a room devoted to this style that won the War, known,

after the brandmark, as Utility. Historically, however, its significance is twofold: it acted upon the national consciousness by re-emphasizing at a popular level the lessons of the Modern Movement; and reaction against its austerities led directly, after the War to the burgeoning of a new romanticism in decoration exemplified notably in the work of John Fowler and Cecil Beaton.

The bedroom of a 'Pre-Fab'. *Neither cheerful curtains nor cheap ornaments can disguise the appalling poverty of design to which the aesthetic of 'modernism' is here reduced. Even the table-lamp, survivor of some pre-war decorative scheme, does as little to raise the spirits as it does to dispel the gloom. You would certainly sleep easy in this bed in the knowledge that democracy was safe, but visually it remains a nightmare.*

OLD LOOK, NEW LOOK

1945 · 1950

THE DEPREDATIONS and deprivations of six years of war taxed the optimism of artists, writers and designers. The creative generation that had added so much to the gaiety of the nation in the 1920s and 1930s responded to conflict and destruction by elegizing a way of life which seemed to them very precious and threatened with extinction. This late flowering of English Romanticism found expression in the paintings of ruins that John Piper made during the Blitz and in the verses of that particularly English poet, John Betjemen, as well as, most eloquently, in Evelyn Waugh's poignant novel of nostalgia for the loss of the English Country House, *Brideshead Revisited* (1945).

Even before the War, John Fowler had begun to assemble the elements of a look which would continue to be lovingly refined throughout the remainder of his long career as a decorator: a style drawn from the most luxurious appointments of the country house and the simplest elements of harness room and kitchen. In reality, Fowler's vision of what he called 'humble elegance' was as much a fictional creation as Waugh's. It is significant, too, that Fowler formed this vision when working in bracing

Mrs Lancaster's Avery Row, Drawing Room, London. Mrs Lancaster became the driving force of Colefax & Fowler during the war, bringing to the firm her feeling for the old houses of Virginia and a love of English grandeur. Her bracing partnership with John Fowler created the English Country House Look as we know it today. Aside from these famous 'butter-yellow' walls such a room would cost as much to recreate as a real Palladian one.

collaboration with his American partner, Nancy Lancaster, who brought to the enterprise a brisk perfectionism not unlike that produced by the collaboration of Edith Wharton and Ogden Codman at the beginning of the century (see page 120).

This classic look was first marketed in the early post-war years by Colefax & Fowler, the firm in which John Fowler had been a partner since 1934. They offered their clients a bold, colourful and richly satisfying blend of the large-scale classicism of William Kent (see pages 47, 48, 51), the sophisticated brilliance of the Regency (see pages 68-77), and the ample comfort of nineteenth-century upholstery (see pages 94, 96): diverse ingredients that nonetheless combined happily in a product as deliciously English as a sherry trifle.

The recipe for this look is straightforward but requires the most careful preparation. Like most modern decorators' styles it is a look intentionally redolent of money and not easily brought off cheaply. Whole bolts of floral glazed chintz go into the making of elaborately swagged or ruched curtain treatments, lavishly hung four-poster beds and in the dressing of tables with multiple layers of drapery and the equipping of every sofa and chair with frilled cushions. The quality of the underlying furniture is of far less importance to the final effect of the room than is the greatest attention to the detailing of upholstery.

Elsewhere the general effect is achieved by a subtle overscaling of considered details, akin to gentle caricature. Broad areas of rush matting are thus enlivened by pretty needlepoint rugs or colourful Oriental carpets, and upholstered seating is counterpointed by consciously eccentric pieces such as a late-eighteenth-century hall chair or a piece of Regency *faux-bamboo*. Here are the origins of many of the details which have become, unfortunately the threadbare clichés of decoration today: the fussy festoon curtain, the heavily fringed pouffe and the too carefully calculated arrangement of tea caddies, patch boxes and other dainty bibelots. The firm that

Madame Yturbe's apartment, Paris. This room, a stylish entrance hall with architectural panelling, was hailed in its day as the decorator's equivalent of Christian Dior's 'New Look'. After the rigours of the German Occupation dress and decoration exploded into a riot of richness and colour. Here the 'New Look' skirt on the table displays the essential fullness of fabric, whilst the tartan carpet is typical of the witty use of materials of the day.

The Drawing Room, Reddish House, Wiltshire. Cecil Beaton, designer, photographer and friend of the famous, created within an exquisite Queen Anne dolls' house this flamboyant salon, which owes everything to flair and nothing to the canons of good taste. Beaton and his decorator Felix Harbord overscaled the objects, many of them reproduction, and played up the French Second-Empire luxuriousness by stretching wine-red velvet on the walls. It is a magnificently 'ham' performance in the old theatrical tradition which Beaton adored.

bears the Fowler name remains the chief exponent of his style, and you may still buy from them the fabrics and papers which he used. Ironically, for it is a direct consequence of his widespread influence, it is possible now to buy in a surprisingly large number of high-street shops materials which are of high quality and convey something of the flavour of his ultimately inimitable style.

The ebullience with which Fowler handled drapery owed much to his intimate knowledge of the trimmings of eighteenth- and nineteenth-century dressmaking, and indeed he was well aware of the sympathetic parallels between his own work and that of the *haute couturiers* of his day. Decorators and dressmakers alike celebrated the newly regained freedom to use fabric lavishly. The New Look, as it was called, originated in Paris in the spring of 1947, and its combination of voluminous skirts and sharply tailored bodices mirrored the lavish fabric treatments but strict architectonic qualities of smart rooms at the beginning of the new decade.

This association of decoration and fashion found its most brilliant exponent in the photographer and designer Cecil Beaton. Before the War his early experiments in decorating had already proclaimed an allegiance to Surrealism and an undoubted predilection for the exotic. However, when he came to decorate Reddish, the house to which he moved in 1947, Beaton was already moving away from the frivolities of dipped plaster drapery and towards a richer, more chic confection of old French furniture, good silks and masses of gilt set against the dark lacquered walls. His taste at Reddish reached its apogee in the creation of a conservatory redolent of the most exotic manifestations of his hothouse tastes. Nowhere – except perhaps in the *coup-de-théâtre* of his black and white Ascot scene for the 1956 production of *My Fair Lady* – did he capture so fully in affectionate parody and broadly effective gesture the combination of period charm and contemporary chic that was the New Look.

FESTIVAL FIFTIES

1951 · 1959

IT WAS IN A SPIRIT of innovation and exploration that the 1951 Festival of Britain was launched. Innovations in science and technology and the exploration of new frontiers of space gave people a strong sense of belonging to a new and exciting age, and this conviction was reinforced in the following year by the accession to the throne of that young Queen who was to give her name to a new Elizabethan era. The romanticism implicit in such a view coloured ideas about technical design, as applied to furnishings and gadgetry in and around the home, so that although the Festival Fifties style is replete with visual reference to molecular models, spaceships and steamlining, it remains no more serious a manifestation of Modernism than a comic strip of Dan Dare.

The Festival was intended to revive national optimism and to serve as a showcase for British design. The styles it proposed were rapidly adopted as part of a new vision of a brighter, more hygienic and egalitarian society. Taking as a starting point the clean lines and economic forms of the International Modernism of the inter-war years, a new generation of designers – including such seminal

Ercol's design for living. In this advertisement roomset Ercol, the manufacturers of that quintessential range of fifties furnishings, bring together diverse traditions to express a new ideal. The use of the traditional Windsor chair as a model together with the emphasis on natural materials reminds us of the Arts and Crafts movement. The use of jazzy colours in bouclé rugs and the asymmetrical placing of a chequer patterned vase speak of a brave new world.

figures as Hugh Casson – rapidly evolved an ornamental aesthetic based on deliberately unhistorical
forms, including chairs and tables with splayed legs,
and new materials such as Formica, more often than
not in primary colours.

There are few, if any, barriers to the achievement
of this essentially democratic look. Most houses or
flats of the post-war period will provide the essentials
of the style: a plain box devoid of architectural
enrichments. The focal point of the room should be
a wall-mounted, chromium-plated, two-bar electric
fire. Even at this late date the heat source remained·
the point about which the room was articulated, with
residual forms of the chimneypiece sometimes
pared down to no more than a shelf of teak or any of
the other Commonwealth woods. Open fires continued to be installed, and a particularly popular
'feature' was the stone-clad chimney breast in which
the opening for the grate was some way up the wall;
this style was derived via the American suburban
home from the simple log-cabin of the Midwest.
Tongued-and-grooved boarding of stained or
natural pine was a more economical variation on a
similar theme which owed its popularity to the widespread influence of Scandinavian design from the
mid-1950s onwards.

The featuring of the chimney breast is a consistent
decorative theme of the period. Walls were almost
invariably white in the most advanced schemes, being
either painted or papered with a textured paper. The

*__The London flat of an American designer.__ Michael
Wolfson took the existing architectural elements of this
converted apartment, renovated in the fifties, and by
giving it a special twist created the first 'tongue-in-
groove' roomset. This brilliant evocation of fifties style
brings together many good designer pieces of the period:
notably a coffee table by Noguchi and chairs by Pierre
Paulin. Notice the raised fireplace. Definitively a room
for someone who likes it hot.*

Objects in a roomscape in Michael Wolfson's flat. The two cone chairs are by Verner Panton and the distinctive glass vase is probably an Italian creation. It stands on a boudoir grand piano which though entirely out of period adds a perfect note of Manhattan sophistication.

chimney breast might then be treated separately in a bold primary colour or with a heavy modernistic embossed wallpaper. The other major notes of colour and pattern would be provided by curtain fabrics, upholstery and carpet. Curtain treatments are austerely plain, being limited almost invariably to straight curtains hanging from track concealed behind plain, rectangular pelmets of plywood or hardboard. Upholstery and some curtains were made from rough and loose-weave fabrics reminiscent of those favoured in the 1930s by Syrie Maugham, but in bright colours. In flooring, the latest look was wall-to-wall broadloom weave carpet,

either plain or with repeating motifs, such as that of the Festival Hall. In kitchens and bathrooms and other areas likely to require a tougher surface, linoleum remained the most usual solution.

Built-in furniture seemed at the time to be the answer to every modern domestic need. Long, low bookcases and cupboards provided at waist height a continuous surface on which lamps and ornaments could be arranged, thus obviating the need for 'fussy' side-tables and shelves. For many middle-class families the Ercol and G-Plan furniture ranges mediated ideally between their more traditional concepts of comfort and an itch for modernity.

The Knoll International style. *The prosperity of the nineteen-fifties revived for designers many of the possibilities and much of the optimism which had first been discovered by the pioneers of 'modernism' in decoration in the thirties. This commercial version of high design uses classic Marcel Breuer chairs and explores the virtues of such favourite modern materials as chrome and tan leather. Note here the return to the luxurious depth of thirties carpeting, which looks forward to the shag-pile of the sixties.*

THE
JET-SET SIXTIES

1960 · 1970

For all the dictates of those twin idols of the period, rational design and a democratic urge towards a simple life, High Style persisted and is still with us. As long as there are international decorators to bring together old furniture and new money there will always be a place for the extravagant gesture. The great exponent of dash with cash is David Hicks, who in the late 1950s and early 1960s brought a quite new and distinctive flair to grand interiors with his bold mixing of old and new elements together with brilliant colouring.

The essence of the Hicks look lies in cleverly matching an eighteenth-century sense of scale with a bravura use of contemporary textiles in saturated and bravely contrasting colours, such as crimson, deep blue and deep violet. Bold geometric patterns emphasize the modernity of the look, while wit and ebullience banish the conventional shibboleths of taste that proscribe the use of, for example, purple tweed on a *fauteuil* signed by a *maître ébéniste* of the reign of Louis XV.

Lighting is of great importance in such rooms. Interesting period light fittings such as an old French *bouillotte* lamp will be used as decorative

An 'Op-Art' room by David Hicks. This drawing room designed in classic Hicks' style played with the black-and-white optical tricks made fashionable in the sixties by the painter Bridget Riley. The black walls strike a daring note and other novel features include hinged metal shutters in the form of screens and Perspex cube coffee-tables. Note the French-style chairs painted stark white and upholstered in geometric weave wool.

Above: The drawing room of Michael Inchbald's London House. Sophistication is the keynote of this room in which grand old objects are combined with clever modern styling. Designed in the late 1950s it is stylistically prophetic of the '60s.
Right: 'Design for the interior of the Markham Arms, Kings Road, Chelsea' by Roderick Gradidge and Anthony Ballantine. When the Kings Road was swinging and fashions were fab 'Victoriana' came back into style as a psychadelic vision in which the peacock feathers of Aestheticism met the sinuous curves of Art Nouveau.

objects in the arrangement of the room, but the drama of these interiors depends upon the skilful use of modern lighting techniques, in particular the employment of uplighters, downlighters and the full range of spotlights.

Perhaps the single most influential contribution of this style to the vocabulary of international decoration has been the 'tablescape', the art of arranging clever, and often valuable objects for rich people on expensive tables.

THE
NEW RURALISM
1968 · 1978

THE GENERATION that grew up under the socialist governments of the 1960s had, in comparison with their parents, vastly expanded horizons and cultural aspirations, both as a result of the democratization of higher education and the hugely increased possibilities of travel. The lifestyle which they created, and which their more commercially minded contemporaries were quick to market, set out deliberately to eschew the traditional signifiers of the English class system, whether grand, suburban or working class. At one level they sought something as simple, wholesome and regenerative as had the

socialists of William Morris's day; this, however, was a culture fed by many tributary streams, and it is fair to say that the cookery books of Elizabeth David and the lyrics of Simon and Garfunkel were no less an influence than the newly revived enthusiasm for all things Pre-Raphaelite.

The 1960s' Earth-Mother made her kitchen the hub of family life, for there all those dreams of an idealized rural existence centred around hearth and home found their fulfilment. Such rooms were based on conventionalized ideas of the farmhouse living room as people fondly imagined it. Holidays

A stripped-pine kitchen by Habitat. More than any other type of room the stripped-pine kitchen living room epitomises the look and attitudes to domestic life of the seventies. The big pine table is reminiscent of the furnishing of traditional kitchens of the nineteenth century and earlier, but here becomes a hub of family activity. Fitted units in natural finish suggest the country, as do earthenware and stoneware crockery. Note the hanging lamp.

spent economically and idyllically in Tuscany or the Dordogne provided not only visual references but a plentiful supply of props such as cheap and attractive earthenware to create the look back at home.

This was the first generation of urban pioneers, who began to reclaim the sound but neglected Victorian building stock so despised by their parents. Large rooms, high ceilings and period details appealed to young couples planning a large family and amused by 'Victoriana'. They set to work, emulsioning walls and ceilings brilliant white and stripping floors and other woodwork only to coat them in polyurethane. The largest room on the ground floor very often became a big 'country-style' kitchen, characteristically dominated by a massive scrubbed-pine table, surrounded by a crazy mix of old and new kitchen and dining-room chairs ranging from Windsor to bentwood and the occasional balloon-back.

This mixing of old and new furniture was part of the fun of the style, at a time when it was still possible to find quirky and interesting antique pieces at reasonable prices and much simple and useful Victorian furniture for almost nothing in second-hand shops. Comfortable and capacious sofas and armchairs were recovered in plain white linen or the cheerful, if inauthentic, reprints of Morris fabrics so heavily promoted by Sanderson at this time. All the most popular printed textiles of the day were derived from the current enthusiasm either for such revived styles as Art Nouveau or for the traditional patterns and colours of India and other Third World countries. From the latter also came the dhurries and kelims which are so much a feature of the look.

In these years the choice of new furniture and a great many other household accessories was largely defined by what was available in Terence Conran's Habitat, the shop that sold the decade. Habitat catered for each of the successive furnishing enthusiasms of the 1960s and 1970s: cheap and cheerful wooden furniture painted in primary colours, natural wood and cane, tubular metal tables and chairs

Above: 'Very Petula Clark…Very Sanderson'. One from a famous series of advertisements promoting the decorative lifestyle of the rich and famous. Petula Clark, the popular singing star, chose a large-scale yellow Sunflower pattern paper typical of its day to give a modern accent to her hideaway in the Swiss Alps.

Right: An art nouveau revival bathroom. Royal blue and pansy purple give a distinctly sixties kick to these over-scaled, re-drawn fin-de-siècle arabesques. Note the coloured bathroom suite and the swept shape of the wash-basin, which has modernistic taps.

and all kinds of shelving units. The store also provided, of course, every essential for the professional Earth-Mother's kitchen.

Every self-regarding 1960s and 1970s household invested in a really big hi-fi system, the various parts of which, disposed about the room and connected by a tangle of wires, may be said to constitute a definitive furnishing statement of the period. The range and variety of lighting available increased enormously, but three forms can now be seen as classic innovations of the era. Simplest, and very nearly universal for a centre light, was the spherical white paper shade which originated in Japan. More directed light was provided by spotlights mounted, usually in twos, on a floor-standing chrome pole. Over tables, hung on a coiled flex, you would almost invariably find one of those plastic dome-shaped shades, which came in white, green, red or in those most associative of period colours, Provençal Donkey or Magic Mushroom.

ALTERNATIVE LIFESTYLES AND OTHER FANTASIES

1955 · 1985

THE IDEA OF A FANTASTICAL interior, created, as Horace Walpole said of his Gothic castle, 'to realize my dreams', is by no means new. From the self-aggrandizing schemes of Renaissance princes, through the wildest chinoiserie flights of fancy of the eighteenth century to those Hollywood visions of a fictional medieval past realized by King Ludwig of Bavaria, the possibilities have been endless – circumscribed only by the limits of imagination or the constraints of income. Even in the twentieth century some brave souls have outfaced convention and created a glamour all their own, as for example did

Cecil Beaton in his merry-go-round of a bedroom in the 1930s at his first house, Ashcombe, in Wiltshire.

By the 1960s a desire to find an 'alternative lifestyle' had become no longer the preserve of a tiny self-consciously bohemian elite, but was increasingly, for all those who thought themselves in any way creative, an essential means of expression. In the public eye such fantasies have become associated with the extravagances of pop stars, fashion designers and other performance artists.

There are no rules in this game, nor any definable boundaries. Such rooms are at their best when they

Zandra Rhodes living-space, London. Something deliberately different from a top designer of the seventies. There is no real furniture; instead amoeba-shaped seating units swirl across the floor covered in Zandra's own whacky fabrics. Conventions like curtains are thrown out of the window in favour of Venetian blinds. The centre of attraction is the television dressed up like a little latter-day shrine.

'The Trip Box' from the exhibition **Designs for Living,** *1969-70. Perhaps the most extraordinary conceptions from a show designed to question all our pre-conceived ideas about living in houses. Alex Mackintyre's Trip Box substituted projected images for reality for the acid generation.*

have a strong theme, such as the obsession with pianos and piano imagery that made the many interiors created by the late Liberace at once ironically witty and opulent. It is worth noting that Liberace bought things because he liked them, not because they were rare and valuable or because conventional fashion and good taste recommended them. This confidence should be the starting point for any collection of objects or interior that seeks to make an individual statement.

In the 1960s one solution to the challenge of creating a truly alternative kind of room lay in abandoning all forms of conventional furniture in favour of bizarre-shaped seating areas in vivid colours scattered across the room like the contents of a tube of Smarties or a pack of M&Ms. A whole cottage industry developed to supply the insatiable demand for decorative objects such as the cut-out palm trees

made for David Hockney and his friends by Mo MacDermott. At a humbler level, the same urge to exhibit one superbly and surrealistically displaced object as the centrepiece of a chaste, minimalist scheme led to vast Javanese kites hanging on the wall or from the centre-light, and to such quirky touches as shop-window mannequins extravagantly decked-out in fancy dress.

From Cecil Beaton's *Fête Champêtre* to Charles de Beistegui's celebrated ball at the Palazzo Labia in Venice in 1951 and the Rothschild Surrealist Ball in the 1960s, fancy dress and fancy decor have gone hand in glove. In more recent years a great professional exponent of this masquerade tradition has been the New Romantic rock-star Adam Ant, who has surrounded himself as a part of his latter-day dandified image with interiors redolent of both Lord Byron and Rudolph Valentino's chic of Araby.

A 'trendy interior'. This room in a late Arts and Crafts style house has been transformed by the introduction of a heterogeneous group of trendy furnishings of the late sixties and early seventies. Inflatable clear plastic chairs were a fashion bubble which soon burst. The Casa Pupo white lamp bases have proved more enduring as have the Portuguese style baroque rugs. Notice the use of two old columns as found ornaments and the huge houseplant.

?

DON'T DREAM IT,
BE IT. . .

Almost every interior of any grandeur in the history of interior decoration started out as someone's fantasy, realized by more or less theatrical means. No matter how conventional the end result may seem to modern eyes, the classical grace of the modest English country house of the eighteenth century sprang first from an obsession with the splendour of ancient Rome, cultivated by the architectural masters of the Renaissance in Italy. Even the discreet charm of the Queen Anne revival houses of Bedford Park depends upon an entirely fictionalized image of Olde England in order to create a pleasant and workaday suburban home.

Since both the humblest and the most pretentious of interiors have provided visual sources for the game of decorating throughout history, do not be frightened of using any style or image to create your own stage-setting. Every style is equally valid, and for each there is a set of rules that defines accurately the period details. But it is the spirit of the style, its theatrical essence that you must seek. We have given you the rules; now go and break them.

A dining room by Anthony Redmile. Anthony Redmile, the sculptor and ingenious designer of rare and bizarre objects here gives his fertile imagination free rein in a fantasy which blends Scottish Baronial, mad Baroque and grand classical elements. Antlers support the table, the chairs and the branches of the chandelier, whilst antique weaponry is arranged in geometric patterns. The vast shell-encrusted busts are favourite Redmile dream objects.

THE DIRECTORY

IN the following pages you will find a directory of manufacturers and suppliers of the products you will need to obtain in order to recreate traditional style interiors. The list makes no claim to be comprehensive, but is intended as a selective introduction to the encouragingly large number of companies who produce high-quality wares, most of whom advertise their services in interior design periodicals and the telephone directory.

Two often related obstacles you may face when attempting to purchase authentic items of period style are scarcity and high cost – regency furniture and Stuart glass being two obvious examples. Whilst you might strike lucky in the auction rooms or antique shops, it is most likely you will have to consider a more available and affordable modern reproduction. However, provided you are discriminating, this can prove to be a very good second best as some of the reproduction pieces now being made do stand comparison with the originals.

Fortunately, many leading companies, notably wallpaper, fabric, china and sanitaryware manufacturers, amongst others, have kept a number of well-known designs in production since their inception in previous centuries. And in response to a rising demand, they have been joined by a new wave of younger companies reproducing traditional wares, especially ceramics, using traditional methods of production. The greater availability of authentic products that has ensued promises it may become increasingly easier to piece together a Traditional Style of your choice.

Hand-painted English Delftware from Isis Ceramics. (For details of stockists see page 214.)

Fabrics Wallpapers *and* Paints

A huge range of original fabric and wallpaper designs from the seventeenth through to the twentieth centuries is available. Many are screen-printed examples of patterns that were originally hand-blocked and have been copied from the original documents. Although they do not quite match the colour and crispness of the originals, they have the advantage of a reasonable price tag. However, hand-blocked fabrics and papers can be purchased, at a price.

Upholstery trimmings from Henry Newbery. (For details of stockists see page 199.)

G.P. AND J. BAKER
Wallpaper and textile manufacturer

For U.K. stockists contact:
18 Berners Street,
London
W1P 4JA.
For U.S. stockists contact:
Payne,
P.O. Box 983,
Dayton,
Ohio, 4540.

Founded in 1884, this company's designs for fabrics and wallpapers are taken from their own archive, started by the brothers George Percival and James Baker over a century ago, containing approximately 2000 samples from the seventeenth to the twentieth centuries. They also produce the National Trust Country House Collection, based on original designs used in English National Trust Houses.

ALEXANDER BEAUCHAMP plc
Wallpaper manufacturer

For U.K. stockists contact:
Griffin Mill,
Thripp, nr Stroud,
Gloucester
GL5 2AZ.

For U.S. stockists contact:
Christopher Hyland Inc.,
Suite 1708,
DND Building,
979 3rd Avenue,
New York.

Specializing in the reproduction of early wallpapers, Alexander Beauchamp often work to commission for bodies such as English Heritage and The Australian National Trust. All products are printed to specification both in colour and design. Designs are available from a large archive of English and French wallpapers, dados, friezes and borders. Ranges include the Archibald Knox collection (1897), and 10 seventeenth century designs.

COLEFAX AND FOWLER
Interior decorators with retail outlets for fabrics and wallpapers.

For U.K. stockists contact:
39 Brook Street,
London
W1Y 2JE.
For U.S. stockists contact:
Cowtan & Tout,
D & D Building,
979 Third Avenue,
New York 10022.

Well-known firm of interior decorators, founded by Lady Sybil Colefax and John Fowler in 1934. John Fowler developed and popularized the English Country House look (see page 000). The company produces wallpapers and fabrics in traditional chintz designs, based on eighteenth and nineteenth century originals.

COLE & SON LTD
Wallpaper and textile manufacturer
By Appointment to H.M. Queen Elizabeth II

For U.K. stockists contact:
18 Mortimer Street,
London
W1A 3BB
For U.S. stockists contact:
Clarence House,
211 East 58th Street,
New York 10022.

Founded in the late 18th century, Cole and Son produce wallpaper and fabrics to designs taken from their own archive, dating back to the 1780s. Products include hand-blockprinted (from some 3000 original blocks) and hand-silkscreen printed items. The firm also manufacture a range of emulsion paints.

HAMILTON-WESTON WALLPAPERS
Wallpaper and textile manufacturer
For U.K. stockists contact:
18 St Mary's Grove,
Richmond-upon-Thames,
Surrey TW9 1UY.
For U.S. stockists contact:
The Rist Corporation,
Washington Design Centre,
Suite 338,
300 Street S.W.
Washington D.C. 20024

Also:
Charles Rupert Designs,
1936 Hampshire Road,
Victoria,
British Columbia,
Canada V8R 5TB.

Hamilton-Weston's designs are taken from their large archive of late seventeenth- to late nineteenth-century English wallpaper documents. There are three ranges: a hand-printed range taken from 1690-1740, a machine-printed range, with screen-printed borders, taken from 1750-1840 and a new range of cotton fabrics. Translations, based on, and designed to co-ordinate with, Regency wallpaper patterns. The U.K. showroom includes a library and other sources of information, as well fabrics and document wallpapers by other manufacturers. The company also offers a comprehensive period design and advice service.

ARTHUR SANDERSON AND SONS
Wallpaper and textile manufacturer

For U.K. stockists contact:
52 Berners Street,
London
W1P 3AD
For U.S. stockists contact:
Sue Morris,
Sanderson,
D & D Building,
197 3rd Avenue,
New York 10022.
Founded in 1860 as an importer of French wallpapers, by the late 1870s the firm was producing its own designs. Today it manufactures a large selection of fabrics and wallpapers taken directly from nineteenth and twentieth century patterns. These are drawn

Morris and Co, hand-painted wallpaper from Sanderson. Trellis design by William Morris, first produced in 1862.

from Sanderson's own archive of some 16,000 textile and wallpaper documents (including original William Morris blocks). Their products are machine-, hand-screen - and block-printed in original colours.

Souvenir D'Afrique (© CS 6142) glazed chintz fabric, from Warner and Sons. Designed by the Silver Studio for Warner's in 1937.

WARNER AND SONS
Wallpaper and textile manufacturer
By Appointment to H.M. Queen Elizabeth II

For U.K. stockists contact:
7-11 Noel Street,
London
W1V 4AL
For U.S. stockists contact:
Warner of London,
c/o Designers Signature,
200 Garden City Plaza,
Garden City,
New York 11530.

Devonshire range
Clarence House,
211 East 50th Street,
New York 10022

Founded in 1870, Warners many fabrics and wallpapers are taken from their enormous archive, which contains their own designs from the 1870s onwards and other nineteenth century pattern books and samples. Their very large range includes: eighteenth century Empire damasks; nineteenth century chintzes (eg. designs from the Chatsworth archive) and English export designs (eg. the Australian collection); early twentieth century chintzes, and eighteenth and nineteenth century Gothic Revival prints.

WATTS & CO LTD
Wallpaper and textile manufacturer

For U.K. stockists contact
7 Tufton Street,
London
SW1 3QB.
For U.S. stockists contact:
Christopher Hyland Inc.,
D & D Building, Suite 1708,
979 Third Avenue,
New York 10022.

Founded in 1874 by three leading architects, G. F. Bodley, Thomas Garner and Gilbert Scott the younger, the firm continues to produce wallpapers, fabrics, trimmings and embroideries from nineteenth-century designs – eg. Bodley's patterns are derived from nineteenth century fabrics and Pugin's Gothic Revival designs. Woven fabrics include silk damasks, cloth of gold etc. Wallpapers are handblocked or silkscreened.

Rose and Coronet wallpaper from Watts and Co. Ltd.

ZOFFANY LTD
Wallpaper and textile manufacturer

For U.K. stockists contact:
63 South Audley Street
London W1Y 5BF.
For U.S. stockists contact:
Twill U.S.A. Ltd,
5100-Highland Park Way,
Cmyrna,
Georgia 30082.

Zoffany manufactures a range of screen - or machine-printed wallpapers to eighteenth century English and French designs, including the Temple Newsan Collection.

JOHN BOYD TEXTILES LTD
Manufacturer of upholstery materials
For U.K. stockists contact:
Higher Flax Mills,
Castle Cary,
Somerset
BA7 7DY.
For U.S. stockists contact:
Scalamandre Silks,
300 Trade Zone Drive,
Ronkonkoma,
New York 11779.

Founded in 1837, this is one of only three
companies in the world making horsehair
fabric, as used by the Victorians for upholstery
top covers.

BRUNSCHWIG & FILS
Textile Manufacturer.

For U.K. stockists contact:
Pallu and Lake,
London Interior Designers Centre,
1 Cringle Street,
London
SW8 5BX.
For U.S. stockists contact:
Brunschwig & Fils,
979 Third Avenue,
New York 10022.
Brunschwig & Fils are an American company
specializing in fabrics from the late eighteenth
and nineteenth centuries. Their designs are
based on original British, French and
American documents.

*Country Bouquet fabric from The Design
Archives. This design dates back to the 1820s.*

THE DESIGN ARCHIVES
Fabric and wallpaper wholesaler

For U.K. stockists contact:
13-14 Margaret Street,
London W1A 3DA.
For U.S. stockists contact:
Clarence House,
211 East 50th Street,
New York 10022

Scalamandre Silks,
300 Trade Zone Drive,
Ronkonkoma,
New York 11779.

A division of Courtaulds plc, the Design
Archives draw on Courtauld's enormous
archive of old designs and pattern books to
produce eighteenth and nineteenth century
document prints on cottons, silks and linens.
They also produce a range of wallpaper
designs.

GAINSBOROUGH SILK WEAVING
COMPANY
Textile manufacturer

For U.K. stockists contact:
Alexandra Road,
Chilton,
Sudbury,
Suffolk
CO10 6XH
For U.S.stockists contact:
Mr P. Hugh Gardner,
P.O. Box 103,
New York NY 10156.

Founded in 1903, Gainsborough's looms use
the original Jacquard mechanism. The
company possesses over 500 Jacquard cards
dating from the sixteenth century, as well as
400 documented fabrics.

CHARLES HAMMOND LTD
Textile designer and manufacturer

For U.K. stockists contact:
253 Fulham Road,
London SW3
For U.S. stockists contact: the above address.

Founded in 1907, Charles Hammond
specialize in a wide range of fabric designs,
based on documents from 1830 through to the
1920s. They also produce handmade
upholstered furniture.

DAVID HICKS INTERNATIONAL
Interior designer with retail outlets for fabrics

For U.K. stockists contact:
4a, Barley Mow Passage,
Chiswick,
London W4 4PH.
For U.S. stockists contact: the above address.

A leading interior designer who came to prominence in the 1960s. The company sells a range of fabrics first designed in that period.

HUMPHRIES WEAVING COMPANY
Textile manufacturer

For U.K. stockists contact:
Devere Mill,
Queen Street,
Castle Hedingham,
Halstead,
Essex CO9 3HA.

This firm produces a wide variety of specialized fabrics suitable for historic interiors, all made to customer's specifications. Seventeenth- to twentieth-century designs available, including a large number of Jacquard designs which are hand-woven on early nineteenth-century Jacquard looms. Commissions include wall fabrics for Ham House, Surrey.

LEE JOFA
Fabric manufacturer

For U.K. stockists contact:
Pallu and Lake,
London Interior Designers Centre,
1 Cringle Street,
London SW8 5BX

For U.S. stockist contact:
Lee Jofa Inc.,
Corporate Headquarters,
800 Central Building,
Carlstadt, NV 07022.

This American company produce designs based on seventeenth- to nineteenth-century English originals.

LIBERTY & CO
Textile manufacturer and retail store

For U.K. stockists contact:
Regent Street,
London
W1R 6AH
For U.S. stockists contact:
229 East 60th Street,
New York 10022.

Founded in 1875 by Arthur Lazenby Liberty, the company continue to produce fabrics from designs commissioned in that period – particularly Art Nouveau and William Morris styles. The shop also stocks antique and reproduction furniture, ceramics and glass, Oriental objects and rugs etc.

IAN MANKIN
Textile retailer

For U.K. stockists contact:
109 Regents Park Road,
London NW1 8UR.

A specialist in natural fabrics eg. raw silk, unbleached calico, muslin, jacquards, mattress ticking, linen and sailcloth. Also sells upholstery fabrics in plain stripes, checks and Indian plaid.

JEAN MONRO
Textile designer and retailer

For U.K. stockists contact:
53 Moreton Street,
London
SW1.
For U.S. stockists contact:
Cowtan & Tout,
D & D Building,
979 Third Avenue,
New York 10022.

Jean Monro sells reprints of eighteenth- and nineteenth-century designs for chintzes as well as a range of hand-blocked linens and cottons and glazed cottons.

H. A. PERCHERON LTD
Textile designer, importer and manufacturer

For U.K. stockists contact:
97-99 Cleveland Street,
London
W1P 5PN.
For U.S. stockists contact: the above address.

The company manufactures a wide range of fabrics such as velvets, damasks, brocades and silks etc. Fabrics and trimmings can also be specially commissioned to customer's requirements. They also import French fabrics and trimmings into the U.K. – particularly fine examples include late eighteenth-century Lyons designs – made by Tassanari and Chatel.

RAMM, SON AND CROCKER LTD
Textile manufacturer

For U.K. stockists contact:
13-14 Treadway Technical Centre,
Treadway House,
Loudwater,
High Wycombe,
Bucks
HP10 9PE.
For U.S. stockists contact:
Brunschwig & Fils,
979 Third Avenue,
New York
10022.

Founded in the mid-nineteenth-century this fabric manufacturer specializes in mainly eighteenth and nineteenth century designs, taken from their own archive of approximately 1,000 documented fabrics.

HENRY NEWBERY
Upholstery trimmings manufacturer

For U.K. stockist contact:
51-55 Mortimer Street,
London
W1
For U.S. stockists contact:
Lee Jafa Inc.,
Corporate Headquarters,
800 Central Building,
Carlstadt,
NV 07022.

Established in 1782, Henry Newbery are the oldest upholstery trimmings manufacturer in England. Their enormous range includes reproduction eighteenth- and nineteenth-century designs.

PRINT ROOM KITS

O'SHEA GALLERY
Dealer in antique prints and maps

For U.K. stockists contact:
89 Lower Sloane Street,
London
SW1 8DA.
For U.S. stockists contact:
Kensington Place Antiques,
80 East 11th Street,
New York
NY 10003.

This gallery, specializing in fifteenth to nineteenth century prints, has revived, using Carolyn Warrender's stencil designs, a similar method of displaying prints and maps to that used in some eighteenth-century printrooms – namely, augmenting them with stencilled frames, bows, borders and swags.

PAINTS

DULUX PAINTS
A Division of ICI.

For U.K. stockists contact:
ICI Paints,
Wexham Road,
Slough,
Berkshire.
For U.S. stockists: contact above address.

Manufacturers of a vast range of high quality paints and glazes. Available in matt, satin and gloss finishes, and retail and trade formulations.

Print room kit from the O'Shea Gallery. Stencilled borders and bows supplement period prints.

Flooring

There is a large number of specialist manufacturers and suppliers of floor coverings who continue to use traditional techniques and materials, such as wool for carpets, rushes for matting, jute and linseed for linoleum etc. For an authentic look, modern, synthetic substitutes simply will not do. Original, and often expensive, rugs and carpets can still be found, but more reasonably priced high-quality reproductions are widely available.

CARPETS
AFIA CARPETS
Carpet retailer

For U.K. stockists contact:
60 Baker Street,
London W1M 1DJ.
For U.S. stockists contact: the above address.

Suppliers of a wide range of traditional body and border carpets. Catalogue available on request.

AXMINSTER CARPETS LTD
Carpet manufacturer

For U.K. stockists contact:
Axminster,
Devon
EX13 5PQ.
For U.S. stockists contact:
Robins Brothers Inc.,
919 3rd Avenue,
New York
10022.

Founded in 1937, this famous manufacturer produces a range of high quality one hundred per cent wool Persian – and Turkish – style carpets.

BOSANQUET IVES
Carpet manufacturer

For U.K. stockists contact:
3, Court Lodge,
48, Sloane Square,
London.

For U.S. stockists: contact the above address.

Suppliers of woven cotton rugs, runners and carpets based on traditional patterns.

HUGH MACKAY PLC
Carpet manufacturer

For U.K. stockists contact:
PO Box 1,
Durham
DH1 2RX.
For U.S. stockists contact:
Hugh Mackay Incorporated,
Suite 1701-1702,
400 Maddison Avenue,
New York 10017.

This company manufactures a wide range of Wilton carpeting – eg. many Persian, Gothic and Art Nouveau inspired designs – plus geometric patterns.

Posy needlepoint carpet from the Vigo Carpet Gallery.

ULSTER CARPET MILLS LTD
Carpet manufacturer

For U.K. stockists contact:
Castleisland Factory,
Portadown,
Craigavon,
N. Ireland.
For U.S. stockists contact:
Landmark Enterprises,
1822a Merchandise Mart,
Chicago,
Illinois 60654.

The Craigavon range includes vivid Art
Nouveau, Art Deco and Persian and Turkish
style patterns.

VIGO CARPET GALLERY
Carpet retailer

For U.K. stockists contact:
6a Vigo Street,
London W1X 1AH.

The shop stocks Oriental and European rugs
and carpets – both original and reproduction
using traditional techniques, eg. Aubusson and
Savonnerie style carpets and Zieglers. They
also stock antique and reproduction textiles.

WOODWARD GROSVENOR
Carpet manufacturer

For U.K. stockists contact:
Stourvale Mills,
Green Street,
Kidderminster,
Worcs,
DY10 1AT.
For U.S. stockists contact: the above address.

Suppliers of body and border carpets (Woven
Wilton and Axminster). They have a unique
library of authenticated designs dating from
the early years of the nineteenth century.

Carpet Fittings
STAIR-RODS U.K. LTD
Brass stair-rod manufacturer

For U.K. stockists contact:
Unit 6,
Park Road,
North Industrial Estate,
Blackhill,
Consett,
Co, Durham
DH8 5UN.
For U.S. stockists contact:
Gripper Rods International PLC,
Blatchford Road,
Horsham,
Sussex
RH13 5QY.

The company supplies solid brass stair-rods
with decorative acorn or ball ends.

Matting

DEBEN RUSH WEAVERS
Manufacturers of rush matting

For U.K. stockists contact:
9 St Peter's Street,
Ipswich,
Suffolk
1P1 1XF.
For U.S. stockists contact: the above address.

The company manufactures a range of
traditional rush matting.

FORBO-NAIRN LTD
Manufacturer of linoleum

For U.K. stockists contact:
P.O. Box 1,
Kirkcaldy,
Fife,
KY1 2SB
Scotland.
For U.S. stockists contact:
Forbo North America Inc.,
1433 Superior Avenue,
No C2,
Newport Beach,
CA-92663.

This company produces linoleum in sheet
and tile form in a variety of plain colours and
patterns.

CAMPBELL MARSON & CO LTD
Specialist in hardwood flooring

For U.K. stockists contact:
36 Maxwell Road,
Fulham,
London
SW6 2HS.
For U.S. stockists contact: the above address.

This firm supplies and lays strip, parquet,
wood block and tongue-and-groove hardwood
flooring.

Lighting

The advances in technology throughout the nineteenth and twentieth centuries have rendered oil and gas lighting all but obsolete, although working oil lamps and gas lights are still available. However, a number of companies supply a wide range of original and high-quality reproduction fixtures and fittings (including chandeliers) that have been converted to run on electricity — without detracting from their appearance.

A hand-crafted, Georgian style Bohemian chandelier, with crystal arms, from Chelsom Ltd.

R. J. CHELSOM & CO LTD
Manufacturers of reproduction lighting

For U.K. stockists contact:
Squires Gate Industrial Estate,
Blackpool,
Lancashire
FY4 3RN.

The company manufactures reproduction light fittings, notably Flemish, Georgian, Regency, Adam, Louis XV and XVI, classical English and Victorian ranges, in polished brass.

CLARE HOUSE LTD
Manufacturer and converter of lamps and lampshades

For U.K. stockists contact:
35 Elizabeth Street,
London
SW1 9RP.
For U.S. stockists contact: the above address.

This prestigious company specializes in the conversion of customer's candlesticks and vases etc into lamps and lampshades. They also stock a range of antique lamps and are employed by the National Trust.

DERNIER & HAMLYN LTD
Manufacturers and Restorers of light fittings

For U.K. stockists contact:
17 Lydden Road,
Wandsworth,
London SW19 4LT.
For U.S. stockists contact: the above address.

Since 1888, the company have been making light fittings which embody the design, craftsmanship and spirit of the eighteenth and nineteenth centuries. Their wide range of lamps and chandeliers includes seventeenth-century Flemish designs. Their lighting, from the standard range or specifically commissioned, can be found in many historic houses – eg. Kensington Palace and the V & A Museum Library, London. Possibly the most skilled restorers in the world of traditional light fittings.

SUGG LIGHTING
Manufacturers of reproduction lighting

For U.K. stockists contact:
Sussex Manor Business Park,
Gatwick Road,
Crawley,
Sussex RH10 2GD
For U.S. stockists contact: the above address.

Founded in 1807, the company manufacture reproduction lighting, using traditional techniques and materials. They produce a wide range of designs, notably from the turn of the century and the 1930s, and specialize in working gas lights. However, electric versions with appropriate brackets and mountings are also available.

CHRISTOPHER WRAY'S LIGHTING EMPORIUM
Lighting retailer

For U.K. stockists contact:
Head Office,
600 King's Road,
London
SW6 2DX.
For U.S. stockists contact: the above address.

The company's 10 branches throughout the U.K. and Ireland stock an enormous range of reproduction light fittings – notably designs from the 1930s as well as from the seventeenth, eighteenth and nineteenth centuries. The emphasis throughout is on quality – eg. solid brass, hand finishing and hand-made glass for 'Tiffany' lamps. The lighting is mainly electric, but they do have some gas and oil lamps as well as a very wide range of accessories. They are also stockists of gold silk Artflex.

Art Nouveau standard lamp from Christopher Wray's Lighting Emporium.

Heating

Original and reproduction fireplaces, mantelpieces, coal-, wood- and oil-burning stoves, and a wide range of accessories are available from manufacturers and suppliers. Many appliances, notably Aga stoves, can be converted to run on electricity without spoiling their appearance. Some of these appliances produce more heat than might be imagined, but you can always box-in radiators or indulge in concealed underfloor heating to supplement warmth and avoid the ghastly appearance of most modern central heating systems.

Edwardian-style cooking range from Elmira Stove and Fireplace.

AMAZING GRATES
Fireplace retailer

For U.K. stockists contact:
Phoenix House,
61-63 High Road,
London N2 8AB.

The company has one of the largest stocks of eighteenth- to twentieth-century fireplaces and mantelpieces (including some Art Deco) in the country. They also stock a wide range of accessories, including Victorian tiles and fire baskets etc.

NIGEL BARTLETT
Dealer in antique chimney pieces

For U.K. stockists contact:
67 St. Thomas Street,
London SE1 7DR.
For U.S. stockists contact:
Above address for photographs.
Shipping arranged.

Dealers in high quality antique chimney pieces in marble, stone and wood. They specialize in the 1740-1820 period, but do have Victorian and Edwardian pieces. Stock is mainly English.

KING'S WORTHY FOUNDRY COMPANY
Manufacturers of cast iron ware

For U.K. stockists contact:
London Road,
King's Worthy,
Winchester,
Hampshire SO23 7QG.
For U.S. stockists contact: the above address.

The company manufactures fine quality period reproduction cast iron fire grates, fire baskets and fire backs etc. and a range of top quality garden furniture.

VERINE
Manufacturer of reproduction fireplaces

For U.K. stockists contact:
Folly Faints House,
Goldhanger,
Maldon,
Essex
CM9 8AP.
For U.S. stockists contact:
Dalton Gorman,
1508 Sherman Avenue,
Everston,
Illinois 60201.

A traditional wood-burning stove from Vermont Castings Inc.

Verine supply reproduction fireplaces to eighteenth and nineteenth century English and French designs – including those by Robert Adam and William Paine – in 'marbellise' and fibreglass. They also supply the 'Verfire' range of gas 'coal' fires.

CLASSIC FURNITURE (NEWPORT) LTD.
Manufacturers of cast iron ware

For U.K. stockists contact:
Audley Avenue,
Newport,
Shropshire TF10 7DS.

Classic Furniture (Newport) Ltd are manufacturers of reproduction Edwardian and Victorian cast iron heaters, stoves, kitchen ranges, fire grates and fire backs etc.

ELMIRA STOVE AND FIREPLACE
Manufacturer of cast iron stoves and cookers

For U.K. stockists contact:
Holden Heat (UK) Ltd,
Court Farm Trading Estate,
Bishops Frome,
Worcester WR6 5AY.

For U.S. stockists contact:
Elmira Stove and Fireplace,
145 Northfield Drive,
Waterloo,
Ontario,
Canada
N2L 5J3.

Elmira are manufacturers of reproduction cast iron wood-burning, solid fuel, gas and electric stoves, ranges and central heating cookers.

AGAHEAT APPLIANCES (BOILERS AND RANGES)
Suppliers of traditional boilers and kitchen ranges

For U.K. stockists contact:
PO Box 30,
Ketley,
Telford,
Shropshire
TF1 1BR.

For U.S. stockists contact:
Coopu and Turner Inc.,
Route 1,
Box 477,
Mountain Road,
Stowe,
Vermont,
Canada 05672.

Suppliers of traditional boilers and kitchen ranges – adapted for gas, electricity or solid fuel. The traditional Aga – a feature of so many English kitchens – was designed in Sweden in 1922, and first reached the U.K. in 1929.

Plasterwork Fixtures *and* Fittings

There is a number of highly reputable companies specialising in architectural salvage and the supply of original fixtures and fittings. Stocks are often extensive and prices range from a few pounds through to telephone numbers, depending on the pedigree, rarity, size etc. of the object in question. Some companies employ teams of skilled craftsmen who will undertake restoration work, and others manufacture high-quality reproductions.

Custom-designed stained glass window from the Victorian Stained Glass Company.

Architectural Fittings

ARCHITECTURAL HERITAGE
Architectural salvage company

For U.K. stockists contact:
Taddington Manor,
Taddington,
Nr Cutsdean,
Cheltenham,
Glos
GL54 5RY
For U.S. stockists contact: the above address.

The company specializes in architectural salvage, including period chimney pieces, panelled rooms and doors in oak, mahogany and pine, carved cornices, columns, stained glass and other decorative items.

CROWTHER OF SYON LODGE
Dealers in architectural salvage and antiques

For U.K. stockists contact:
Busch Corner,
London Rd,
Isleworth,
Middx
TW7 5BH.
For U.S. stockists contact: the above address.

Dealers in architectural antiques, specializing in panelled rooms, chimney pieces, ironwork, marble and bronze statuary and garden ornaments. They have their own restoration team of carpenters and stonemasons.

T. CROWTHER AND SON
Dealers in architectural salvage and antiques

For U.K. stockists contact:
282 North End Road,
London
SW6 1NH.
For U.S. stockists contact: the above address.

Founded in 1882 in a large, late Georgian period building, the company's large showrooms display fine Georgian panelling, chimney pieces and fire accessories, furniture, wall lights and chandeliers.

THE LONDON ARCHITECTURAL SALVAGE AND SUPPLY COMPANY
Supplier of original architectural fixtures and fittings

For U.K. stockists contact:
Mark Street,
London
EC2A 4ER.

For U.S. stockists contact:
Nostalgia,
307 Stiles Avenue,
Savannah,
Georgia
31401.

LASSCO stock doors, panelling, staircases, fireplaces, ironwork, baths basins and accessories, slate and quarry tiles, skirting, floorboards, window frames, leaded and stained glass etc. They specialize in woodwork (including decorative architectural carvings) and ironmongery.

ROBERT MILLS LTD
Supplier of original architectural fixtures and fittings

For U.K. stockists contact:
Unit 3,
Satellite Business Park,
Blackswarth Road,
Bristol,
Somerset
BS5 8AX.
For U.S. stockists contact: the above address.

Suppliers of architectural antiques and decorative fittings, with particular emphasis on 'the dramatic, the ornate and the flamboyant'. Monumental and smaller items are available. They specialize in Victorian and Edwardian (including Gothic Revival) items – most notably a large stock of nineteenth- and twentieth-century stained glass.

MARTIN OAKLEY
Panelling, door and mantelpiece manufacturer

For U.K. stockists contact:
24 Warnborough Road,
Oxford,
Oxfordshire
OX2 6JA.
For U.S. stockists contact: the above address.

Panelled rooms made to order – eg. libraries, bathrooms and drawing rooms. Eighteenth- and nineteenth-century style doors and mantelpieces.

BRASS AND IRON FITTINGS

J. D. BEARDMORE & CO. LTD
Suppliers of brass and iron fittings

For U.K. stockists contact:
P.O. Box 2,
300 Crownpoint Road,
Glasgow G40 2UP.
For U.S. stockists contact: the above address.

The company supplies reproduction door and cabinet fittings (in brass and black iron), brass curtain poles and accessories, brass grilles (eg. for radiator casements) and brass luggage racks (eg. for the Orient Express).

COMYN CHING LTD
Supplier of brass and iron fittings
For U.K. stockists contact:
110 Golden Lane,
London EC1Y 0SS.
For U.S. stockists contact: the above address.

Brass and black iron door furniture, handles, pulls and hinges.

B. LILLY & SONS LTD
Suppliers of brass and iron fittings

For U.K. stockists contact:
Baltimore Road,
Birmingham B42 1DJ.
For U.S. stockists contact: the above address.

Manufacturers of interior metal fittings in nineteenth and twentieth century designs. The 'Antique' range of cabinet handles is produced from patterns used for over 100 years.

G. J. GREEN & VERONESE
Specialists in plasterwork, decorative mouldings, gilding and murals

For U.K. stockists contact:
Interior House,
Lynton Road,
Cromer End,
London N8 8SL.
For U.S. stockists contact: the above address.

Specialists in plasterwork, gilding and murals etc. They carry a large stock of cornices and mouldings, and also undertake restoration work.

THE VICTORIAN STAINED GLASS CO.
Stained glass studio

For U.K. stockists contact:
83 Stamford Hill,
London N16 5TP.
For U.S. stockists contact: the above address.

This company design and make stained, leaded, bevelled, brilliant cut and acid-etched glass to customers' specifications for windows and other fixtures.

Kitchens

Whilst it might be aesthetically pleasing to recreate an authentic pre-1830 kitchen, it would also be ergonomically insane. Which is why most owners of pre-Victorian homes prefer to create either a pastiche of an earlier style, a Victorian kitchen or a dateless country-style room, in which fridges, freezers, microwaves etc. are hidden away behind cupboard doors. There are a number of reputable companies who can design and install 'unfitted' or 'fitted' kitchens to meet your requirements.

Bleached oak dresser from Smallbone and Co.

JOHN LEWIS OF HUNGERFORD
Kitchen manufacturer

For U.K. stockists contact:
Unit 2,
Limborough Road,
Wantage,
OX12 9AJ.
For U.S. stockists contact: the above address.

Manufacturer and installer of a wide range of solid wood fitted and unfitted kitchen furniture.

ROBINSON & CORNISH
Handmade kitchen manufacturer

For U.K. stockists contact:
The Old Tannery,
Hannaford Lane,
Swimbridge,
Devon
EX32 0PL.
For U.S. stockists contact: the above address.

Specialists in handmade kitchen units for fitted kitchens and individual pieces for unfitted kitchens. The company also stocks a range of high quality Victorian style sinks, taps and various accessories.

SMALLBONE & CO (DEVISES) LTD
Designers, maufacturers and installers of kitchens and bathrooms

For U.K. stockists contact:
105-109 Fulham Road,
London
SW3
For U.S. stockists contact:
Smallbone Incorporated,
A & D Building,
150 East 58th St,
New York
10155.
and:
315 South Robertson
Boulevard,
Los Angeles.

Well known specialists in traditional kitchen, bathroom and bedroom furniture. Their products are made by skilled craftsmen in a variety of woods including oak and pine. They can recreate eighteenth-, nineteenth- and twentieth-century period detailing, offer a wide range of hand-painted finishes and carry out complete installations to individual customer's specifications. They also offer a comprehensive design service.

STUDIO TWO (INTERIOR DESIGN) LTD.
Interior Designers specializing in restoration and recreation of English period kitchens.

For U.K. stockists contact:
3a Town Street,
Thaxted,
Essex,
CM6 2LD.
For U.S. stockists contact: the above address.

This company specializes in the restoration and/or recreation of English period kitchens, hearths and inglenooks etc. Restoration covers joinery, brickwork, flooring etc. Specialist craftsmen are used to recreate furniture, fittings, finishes etc.

Cookers
HOLDEN HEAT PLC
Suppliers of cast iron cooking ranges

For U.K. stockists contact:
Court Farm Trading Estate,
Bishops Frome,
Worcestershire
WR6 5AY.
For Canadian stockists contact:
Elmira Stove and Fireplace,
145, Northfield Drive,
Waterloo,
Ontario,
Canada.

Supplier of reproduction nineteenth century, cast iron cooking ranges which can be run on electricity, gas or a combination of solid fuel and electricity.

For further information regarding cooking ranges: see page 205.

Accessories
ELIZABETH DAVID LTD
Retailer of kitchen equipment

For U.K. stockists contact:
46 Bourne Street,
London
SW1 8DJ.
For U.S. stockists contact:
Bloomingdales of New York.

Suppliers of high quality traditional kitchen ware such as copper moulds and saucepans, horn spoons and cast iron scales.

English oak fitted kitchen from Smallbone and Co., featuring an Aga cooking range (for details of Aga stockists see page 205).

Bathrooms *and* Ceramic Tiles

Due to ever-increasing demand, many of the sanitary ware manufacturers who have been trading since the end of the nineteenth century have continued to produce most of their traditional ranges designed between the 1870s and the 1930s. That same demand has seen ceramic tile manufacturers and suppliers increase their ranges of high-quality reproduction tiles, many of which are hand-painted and produced using traditional methods. Originals can still be found, but obviously are more expensive.

Victorian wall and floor tiles from the Art Tile Company provide a backdrop to a typical reproduction, cast-iron, roll-top bath.

BATHROOMS
ADAMSEZ
Sanitary ware manufacturer

For U.K. stockists contact:
Adamsez Ltd.,
Dukerway
Team Valley Trading Estate,
Gateshead,
Tyne and Wear NE11 0SW.
For U.S. stockists contact: the above address.

Established over 100 years ago, this company manufactures traditional bathroom ware, including the 'Westbury' – the only Art Deco suite in Britain still to be manufactured in original 1930s fire clay by craftsmen. Victorian and Edwardian styles are also made – such as the Victoriana, first manufactured in 1870, and the Imperial.

ARMITAGE SHANKS LTD
Sanitary ware manufacturer

For U.K. stockists contact:
Armitage,
Old Road,
Rugeley,
Staffordshire WS15 4BT.
For U.S. stockists contact: the above address.

This firm dates from Victorian times and still manufactures traditional ranges of sanitary ware, including the 'Clarendon', 'Carlton', 'Victorian', 'Wentworth' and 'Kensington' suites. The 'Dolphin' suite – their prize-winning design in the Great Philadelphia Exhibition of 1876 – has just been re-introduced. This suite features decorative cast iron brackets for the cistern, a washstand with mahogany doors, and a w.c. shaped like a shell and supported by a dolphin. The firm also manufactures traditional butler's/Belfast sinks for kitchens.

ORIGINAL BATHROOMS
Manufacturer and retailer of bathroom fixtures and fittings

For U.K. stockists contact:
143-145 Kew Road,
Richmond,
Surrey TW9 2PN.

Importers and manufacturers of a wide range of traditional bathroom suites, including the 'Palladio' and 'Belle Epoque' ranges, the company is run by the descendants of Frederick Humpherson, who designed the original pedestal wash-down watercloset – 'The Beaufort' – in the 1880s.

B. C. SANITAN LTD
Sanitaryware manufacturer

For U.K. stockists contact:
12 Nimrod Way,
Reading,
Berkshire RG2 0EB.
For U.S. stockists contact:
Besco Sales Corporation,
729 Atlantic Avenue,
Boston,
Mass. 02111.

Manufacturer of high quality sanitaryware and accessories in Victorian and Art Deco styles.

BLACK COUNTRY HERITAGE
Manufacturer of bathroom accessories

For U.K. stockists contact:
11-12 Landport Industrial Estate,
Wolverhampton
WV2 2QJ.
For U.S. stockists contact:
Coyne Electrical Inc.,
298, East 149th St.,
New York NY 10451.

Specialist manufacturers of high quality brass bathroom accessories – including heated towel rails – based on traditional designs.

TILES
THE ART TILE COMPANY LTD
Manufacturer of ceramic tiles

For U.K. stockists contact:
The Etruria Works,
Garner Street,
Etruria,
Stoke-on-Trent,
Staffs ST4 7SB.

London office and showroom:
The Tileworks,
Studio 10,
39 Tadema Road,
London
SW10 0PY.
For U.S. stockists contact:
Country Floors,
300 East 61st Street,
New York
10021.

Also:
Shep Brown Associates,
307 West 1st Street,
South Boston
MA 02127.

This young company combine traditional techniques with the latest technology in order to produce the highest quality tiles in their own designs, along with reproduction work. They stock a Victorian collection, plus other designs from the nineteenth to early twentieth centuries.

CERAMIC TILE DESIGN
Designers and manufacturers of ceramic wall and floor tiles

For U.K. stockists contact:
56 Dawes Road,
Fulham,
London SW6
For U.S. stockists contact: the above address.

Specialist in unusual imported and hand-decorated tiles. The company can provide patterns ranging from antique Delft and 18th century Spanish through to Victorian and 20th century styles.

FIRED EARTH
Designers and manufacturers of ceramic wall and floor tiles

For U.K. stockists contact:
Middle Aston,
Oxon OX5 3PX.
For U.S. stockists contact: the above address.

Producers of craftsman-made ceramic tiles using centuries-old methods and techniques. Range includes English delft, and quarry styles.

For further tile manufacturers see Bathrooms, page 000.

MAW & CO. LTD
Manufacturer of ceramic tiles

For U.K. stockists contact:
H. & R. Johnson Tiles Ltd,
Highgate Tile Works,
Tunstall,
Stoke-on-Trent,
Staffordshire
ST6 4JX.
For U.S. stockists contact:
H. & R. Johnson Inc.,
P.O. Box 23,
Keyport,
New Jersey
07735.

Manufacturer of reproduction Victorian and Edwardian tiles, many of which are based on designs first produced at the turn of the century for their Minton Hollins range – this includes plain, moulded and patterned tiles and borders. They undertake commissions for hand painted and tubelined ceramic panels and murals as well as restoration work.

Furniture

Most, perhaps all, of the furniture shown in this book can be purchased at auction or in antique shops. However, some pieces, notably Regency, are so expensive, and others, such as Rococco and Gothick, so rare, that you may, through consideration of time and money, have to purchase a reproduction piece. But don't despair, because there is an increasing number of companies who manufacture and supply quality reproduction furniture that stands comparison with the originals.

Kelim-covered chair from George Smith, made using traditional methods and fabrics.

ERCOL
Manufacturers of twentieth century furniture

For U.K. stockists contact:
London Road,
High Wycombe,
Bucks HP13 7AE
For U.S. stockists contact:
The Happy Viking,
Grantz Plaza,
Route 206 South,
Ravitan,
New Jersey 08869.

The company manufactures stylish fifties through to contemporary design furniture.

SIMON HORN
Classical wooden bed specialist

For U.K. stockists contact:
117-121 Wandsworth Bridge Road,
London
SW6 2TP

This company retail period style wooden beds, mostly handmade in France in traditional designs such as Lit Bateau and Empire. They also sell traditional English furniture such as pedestal desks and butler's trays.

PARKER KNOLL
Manufacturers of twentieth century classic furniture

For U.K. stockists contact:
The Courtyard,
Frogmoor,
High Wycombe,
Bucks HP13 50JJ.
For U.S. stockists contact: the above address.

This company manufactures twentieth century classic furniture – such as the Breuer chair – in high quality materials. They also offer a comprehensive restoration service.

GEORGE SMITH
Manufacturers of traditional furniture

For U.K. stockists contact:
587-589 Kings Road,
London SW6 2EH.
For U.S. stockists contact:
Howard Kaplin Antiques,
827 Broadway,
New York NY 10003.

The company manufactures sofas and chairs, hand made and embellished in the manner of the nineteenth century, and specializes in opulent, kelim covers.

TUDOR OAK
Manufacturer of traditional oak furniture

For U.K. stockists contact:
Bakers Cross,
Cranbrook,
Kent
TN17 3AL.
For U.S. stockists contact: the above address.

The company produces high quality range
handmade, oak reproduction furniture, based
on sixteenth-, seventeenth- and eighteenth-
century design.

*Knole sofa from George Smith, craftsman-
made with solid beechwood frame and real
horsehair, feather and down stuffing.*

*Lit–Bateau from Simon Horn. A handmade,
French style, hardwood daybed.*

China, Silver *and* Glass

A number of manufacturers has kept various well-known ceramic designs in production for more than two hundred years – much of which is still hand-painted, rather than transfer-printed. A few manufacturers of silver and plate continue to produce flatware in eighteenth and nineteenth century designs, and it is still possible to find specialist craftsmen who produce hand-blown glass in traditional designs. The alternative is to look in auction houses and antique shops.

Royal Albert Bone China from Royal Doulton Ltd.

CLASSICAL CREAMWARE LTD
Manufacturer of traditional pottery

For U.K. stockists contact:
6 Redworth Way,
Newton Aycliffe,
Co. Durham
For U.S. stockists contact:
Macey's stores.

Faithful reproductions of eighteenth century creamware pottery, including dinner services and domestic ware such as ewer and basin sets, shaving mugs, ink wells and candle holders.

ISIS CERAMICS
Pottery

For U.K. stockists contact:
The Old Toffee Factory,
120A Marlborough Road,
Oxford.
For U.S. stockists contact:
Barneys, Gumps or Hendi Bendel Stores.

Unique, hand-potted and painted dinner sets, jugs and bowls drawn from original seventeenth- and eighteenth-century English Delftware.

ROYAL DOULTON (U.K.) LTD.
Manufacturer of traditional china

For U.K. stockists contact:
Hobson Street,
Burslem,
Stoke-on-Trent,
Staffordshire
ST6 2AW.
For U.S. stockists contact:
PR Department,
Royal Doulton USA Inc.,
Cottontail Lane,
Somerset,
New Jersey
08873.

*Royal Doulton:*traditional ranges still in manufacture include variations of the 'Willow' pattern originally produced in 1820, and 'Flora Dora' from the 'Majestic' collection – a floral pattern of the late nineteenth century.
*Royal Albert:*early twentieth-century designs still in manufacture include: 'Lady Carlyle' (since 1927, and modified in 1946), 'Lady Hamilton' (since 1939), 'Petit Point' (1932), 'Heirloom' (since 1915, and modified in the 1930s), 'Blossomtime' (since 1935), 'American Beauty' (since 1938) and the 'Silverbirch' (since 1940).
*Minton:*some nineteenth and early twentieth

century dinner services still made – eg. 'Cuckoo' (since 1830), 'The Cockatrice' (since 1840), 'Minton Rose' (since 1860), 'Dynasty' (since 1925), 'Marlow' (since 1938), 'Riverton' (since 1928) and 'Ancestral' (since 1938). *Royal Crown Derby:* traditional lines of fine china still in production include: 'Old Imari' (since 1880), 'Traditional Imari' (since 1888), 'Kings Pattern' (since 1920), 'Asian Rose' (since 1910), 'Brittany' (since 1880), 'Blue Mikado' (since 1892) and 'Posie' (since the 1930s).

ROYAL WORCESTER PORCELAIN WORKS
China manufacturer

For U.K. stockists contact:
7 Severn Street,
Worcester,
Worcestershire
WR1 2NE.
For U.S. stockists contact:
Royal Worcester Spode,
26, Kennedy Boulevard,
E. Brunswick,
New Jersey 08816.
Also:
Royal Worcester Spode USA
Suite 6a
41, Maddison,
New York 10010.

Founded in 1751, many of their traditional lines are no longer produced – except for 'Imperial' (c.1910), a blue or white service with a heavy hand gilded pattern, the 'Blue/Royal Lily' (eighteenth-century) and individually commissioned crested services.

JOSIAH WEDGWOOD & SONS LIMITED
Manufacturer of fine bone china

For U.K. stockists contact:
Barlaston,
Stoke-on-Trent,
Staffordshire ST12 9ES.
For U.S. stockists contact:
Waterford Wedgewood USA Inc.,
PO Box 1454,
Wall,
New Jersey 07719.

Founded in 1759, the company continues to produce many of its eighteenth- and nineteenth-century designs. Their original

Osborne. A typically English 'high-tea' design (named after Queen Victoria's residence on the Isle of Wight) from Josiah Wedgwood and Sons Ltd.

pattern books are an important design source for the studio.

CUMBRIA CRYSTAL LTD.
Glass manufacturers

For U.K. stockists contact:
Lightburn Road,
Ulverston,
Cumbria
LA12 0DA.

Manufacturers of fine full-lead English crystal, based on seventeenth- and eighteenth-century designs. The glass is hand-blown and the perfect pieces sold as first quality clear crystal – the only company in England to produce this. Other glass is decorated by highly-skilled cutters, employing patterns going back to the seventeenth century.

NAZEING GLASS WORK LTD.
Glass manufacturer

For U.K. stockists contact:
Nazeing New Road,
Broxbourne,
Hertfordshire
EN10 6SU.
For U.S. stockists contact: the above address.

This company dates back to a seventeenth century glasshouse in Vauxhall, London. They produce a wide range of glass, including some reproduction ware – eg. Bristol Blue glass (1780-1830). Much of their work is to special commission – but for small batches rather than one-off pieces.

Silverware
MAPPIN & WEBB
Manufacturer of silver and plate; retailer of silver, plate glass and china

For U.K. stockists contact:
170 Regent Street
London
W1R 6BQ.
For U.S. stockists contact: the above address.

Established in 1774, Mappin and Webb still produce flatware to their eighteenth- and nineteenth-century designs. Products include cutlery, candelabra, cruet sets, tea and coffee pots.

Mappin Plate Octagonal tea service and a Mappin Plate bud base. (A contemporary reproduction of a traditional nineteenth century design.)

Bristol Blue glass from the Nazeing Glass Company.

GLOSSARY

Andiron
An iron bar used to support the end of a log in a fire.

Anthemions
Honeysuckle or palm-like ornamentation.

Architectonics
The science of architecture.

Arcading
A row of open or closed arches supported on columns or pilasters, usually forming a covered passageway.

Abusson and Savonerie-type patterns
Respectively, flat-weave and tapestry carpets, made for the European market at the French Royal Carpet factories. Also, carpets made in the style of these factories.

Bakelite
A heavy, durable synthetic resin (invented by L.H. Baekeland) most commonly moulded to form, amongst other objects, early telephones and radio casings.

Bauhaus
A German school of design founded by the architect Walter Gropius in 1919. Design and construction were related to the needs of function and machine construction, resulting in predominently box-like forms, straight lines and an absense of all but strictly geometric decoration. Notable practitioners included Paul Klee, Marcel Breuer, Wassily Kadinsky and Laszlo Moholy-Nagy.

Biedermerer
An essentially bourgeois style of furniture, interior decoration and Bohemian glass and porcelain that first appeared in Austria and Germany after the Napoleonic wars. The furniture was mostly hand-crafted in walnut and softwoods such as cherry and pear, and displayed geometric forms and, often, sophisticated motifs.

Boiseries
Wood panelling.

Bolection moulding
A decorative moulding constructed around, and projecting beyond, a panel.

Bouillotte lamp
A lamp used to illuminate a card table. (*Bouillotte* was a French game similar to poker.)

Brocatelle
A stiff, heavy-figured, silk-and-linen fabric.

Bullion thread
A heavy-weight twisted cord, covered in gold or silver wire, used in fringing.

Cabriole legs
Outwardly curving legs deployed on drawing- and dining-room chairs, notably from 1830-1880, and often combined with a balloon back.

Caryatid
A female figure deployed in place of a column to support an entablature.

Cloak-pin tiebacks
Circular curtain tie-back, usually of ornamental gilt metal, attached to the wall by a turned stem. The curtain may be draped behind the tie-back or wound round it.

Corona
A 'crown' or ring, usually of metal, forming the chief structural member of a light fitment, or the support of bed-drapery.

Crackle-glaze
A varnish specifically formulated to crack and craze as it dries out, thereby simulating the effects of weathering and ageing on painted or stained surfaces.

Cretonnes
A boldly printed fabric suitable for curtains and upholstered furniture.

Dado
A skirting or rail, usually of wood, running around the walls of a room at approximately the height of a chair back, and the space below that rail and above the skirting board.

Dhurrie
An Indian cotton carpet, usually with fringing.

Famille rose and famille verte
Chinese porcelain (of the Chien Lung Dynasty) on which pink and green hues are prominent in the pattern.

Fauteuil
A French armchair.

Faux bamboo and faux marbre
'Fake' bamboo and marble, created by embellishing plain wooden or plaster surfaces with translucent paints and glazes to simulate the appearance of the natural materials.

Fillet
A moulding, usually of gilded wood, sometimes metal fretwork, used as a trim for wall coverings or panels of stretched fabric.

Finials
Ornamental foliage on top of a gable.

Fire-dogs *see Andirons.*

Fish-tails
The folded hanging drapery of a pelmet, falling in overlapping loops. The lining of the curtain material, revealed by the folds is often in a contrasting colour.

Flat colour
A high quality matt finish paint or glaze. Not as hardwearing as eggshell or gloss finish paints and glazes.

Garnitures
Sets of ornaments (such as vases) which embellish a surface or setting.

Gesso
A plaster of Paris used to prepare a smooth surface for painting.

Gothick
Eighteenth and early nineteenth century spelling of Gothic, denoting today the delicate applied ornament which was fashionable before the full-scale Gothic Revival of 1840 onwards.

Kelim
Waren, flat carpet, with geometric patterns, produced chiefly in Turkey. The patterns come in distinctive colourways eg. Pink, acid green and black.

Linoleum
Durable floor covering made from fabric (often jute) impregnated with resins, linseed oil and fillers (such as cork). Available in a variety of colours and (random) patterns. Not to be confused with vinyl flooring.

Lit à la Polonaise
A French bed-style of the 1780s, imported into England. Set side to the wall, the bed is draped with curtains and snags, supported from a dome or 'corona' above.

Lit-en-bateau
Literally a 'boat-bed', it has scrolled head and footboards of equal height, sometimes ornamented with ormolu mounts.

Lustres
A candlestick or vase ornamented with pendants of cut-glass.

Maitre ebeniste
A master ebonist. (Ebonise: to make another wood look like ebony.)

Mezzotint
A method of copperplate engraving that produces an even gradation of tones.

Moquette
A canvas-backed furnishing fabric with a thick-cut velvet pile.

Ormolu
Pale yellow gilt or bronzed metallic ware, normally covered with a protective coat of clear lacquer.

Parian-ware
A type of porcelain that looks like fine marble.

Passementerie
Decorative trimming.

Passe-partout
A simple picture frame (usually made from pasteboard); the picture being fixed in position by strips of adhesive tape or paper pasted over the edges.

Paterae
Round flat ornaments, such as rosettes, that usually appear as bas-relief in friezes etc.

Pilaster
A square column built into, and partly projecting from, a wall.

Purdonium
A coal-scuttle/bucket.

Register plate
A device on the front of a fire-grate that enables the draught to be regulated.

Rep (woollen)
Corded cloth.

Rim-lock
A cased lock fitted to the wooden frame of a door.

Rococo
The style popularised first in France, in the 1720s 'rocaille' or shell decoration. Rococo is a nonsense word, which embraces shell, foliage, swept and delicately curved forms of all kinds.

Scagliola
A man-made stone, consisting of stone chippings bound together in a mixture of cement.

Singerie
'Monkey-business', or scenes involving monkeys often dressed in human clothing. An anthropomorphic theme popular in eighteenth century decoration.

Solar chambers
The private upper chamber, reserved for the master and mistress, and found in early 'hall houses'.

Spill-holder
A container for small strips or tapers of wood and paper used to light fires, candles, pipes etc.

Strapwork
An ornamentation of crossed and interlaced fillets.

Terrazzo
A polished mosaic covering for concrete floors, consisting of marble and/or stone chips set in cement.

Tracery
Surface ornamentation of intersected, flowing lines most commonly associated with Gothick architecture.

Watts moulding
A formalised foliate motif cast in plaster, used extensively in late nineteenth and early twentieth century framing. Named after its designer, the painter George Frederick Watts.

BIBLIOGRAPHY
⧽⧽⧼⧼

Elizabeth Aslin: *The Aesthetic Movement* Studio Vista

Elizabeth Aslin: *Victorian Furniture* Studio Vista

Martin Battersby: *The Decorative Twenties* Herbert Press

Martin Battersby: *The Decorative Thirties* Herbert Press

Geoffrey Beard: *Craftsmen and Interior Decoration in England, 1660-1820* Bloomsbury Books

Stephen Calloway: *Twentieth Century Decoration* Weidenfeld & Nicolson (UK), Rizzoli (USA)

John Cornforth: *English Interiors, The Quest for Comfort, 1790-1848* Barrie & Jenkins

Caroline Davidson: *The World of Mary Ellen Best* Chatto & Windus

Terence Davis: *The Gothick Taste* David & Charles

Ralph Edwards: *Dictionary of English Furniture* Country Life

John Fowler & John Cornforth: *English Decoration in the 18th Century* Barrie & Jenkins

Philippe Garner: *Twentieth-Century Decoration* Phaidon

Ian Grant (ed.) *Great Interiors* Studio Vista

Mark Girouard: *Life in the English Country House* Yale University Press

David Hicks: *On Living-With Taste.* Leslie Frewin

Hugh Honour: *Chinoiserie* John Murray

Thomas Hope: *Household Furniture and Interior Decoration* Academy

Christopher Hussey: *Early Georgian Country Houses* *Mid-Georgian Country houses* *Late Georgian Country Houses* Antique Collectors' Club

Stephen Jones: *Ackermann's Regency Furniture and Interiors*

Margaret Jourdain: *English Interior Decoration, 1500-1830* Batsford

Lionel Lambourne: *Utopian Craftsmen* Astragal

Osbert Lancaster: *A Cartoon History of English Architecture* John Murray

Susan Lasdun: *Victorians at Home* Weidenfeld & Nicolson

Charles Oman: *Wallpapers* Sothebys

Mario Praz: *An Illustrated History of Interior Decoration* Thames & Hudson

Peter Thornton: *Seventeenth-Century Interior Decoration in England, France and Holland* Yale University Press

Peter Thornton: *Authentic Decor, 1620-1920* Weidenfeld & Nicolson

Mark Turner: *The Silver Studio of Design* Webb & Bower

David Watkin: *The Royal Interiors of Regency England* J.M. Dent

Ray Watkinson: *Pre-Raphaelite Art and Design* Studio Vista

Edith Wharton & Ogden Codman: *The Decoration of Houses* Norton

INDEX

ACKNOWLEDGEMENTS

6 Christopher Wood Gallery, London; **8** Philip de Bays; **10** Reproduced by gracious permission of Her Majesty the Queen; **11** Lt. Col. Stuart Chart-Sempill; **12** Museum of London/Locke; **13** Private Collection; **14** Angus McBean; **17** National Portrait Gallery, London; **18** The World of Interiors/Christopher Simon-Sykes; **19** National Trust Photographic Library/ Eric Chrichton; **20** The World of Interiors/Tom Leighton; **21** Angus McBean; **22** The World of Interiors/Lucinda Lambton; **24/25** National Trust/Knole; **26** By courtesy of the Board of Trustees of the Victoria & Albert Museum; **28** Tate Gallery, London; **29** National Trust/Knole; **33** National Trust Photographic Library/ John Bethell; **36** Philip de Bays; **38** National Trust Photographic Library; **41 right** By courtesy of the Board of Trustees of the Victoria & Albert Museum; **41 left** By kind permission of Country Life; **43** National Trust Photographic Library/Angelo Hornak; **44** Dennis Severs/ Tim McManus; **46** English Heritage; **47** Reproduced by courtesy of the Board of Trustees, The National Gallery, London; **49** Yale Center for British Art, The Paul Mellon Collection; **50** National Trust Photographic Library/ Andrew Haslam; **52** National Trust Photographic Library/ Mark Fiennes; **55** Courtesy of the Lewis Walpole Library, Yale University; **56** National Trust Photographic Library; **58** Marquess of Zetland; **59** Stephen Calloway; **60** National Trust Photographic Library/John Bethell; **63** Courtesy of the National Gallery of Ireland; **64** National Trust Northern Ireland Region; **67** By courtesy of the Board of Trustees of the Victoria & Albert Museum; **68** Royal Pavillion, Art Gallery and Museums, Brighton; **70** By kind permission of Country Life; **71** Reproduced courtesy of Cameron Books; **72/73** Angelo Hornak; **76** By courtesy of the Trustees of Sir John Soames Museum; **78** The Duke of Wellington; **81** By courtesy of the Board of Trustees of the Victoria & Albert Museum; **82** York City Art Gallery; **83** From 'The World of Mary Ellen Best' Caroline Davidson, reproduced by courtesy of Chatto & Windus; **87** Tate Gallery, London; **88** Macdonald Orbis Archive; **90** National Trust Photographic Library/Michael Boys; **91** The National Trust Photographic Library/Rob Matheson. Reproduced courtesy of the Marquess of Northampton; **93** English Heritage; **94** By Kind permission of Country Life; **97** From 'English Style' Suzanne Sleslin & Stafford Cliff (Thames & Hudson). Photo: Ken Kirkwood; **98** National Trust Photographic Library/Rob Matheson; **99** Trustees of the Science Museum; **100** National Trust Photographic Library; **102** Courtesy of Sotherbys, Private Collection; **103** Macdonald Orbis Archive; **104** The British Architectural Library, RIBA, London; **105** From 'English Style' Suzanne Sleslin & Stafford Cliff (Thames & Hudson). Photo: Ken Kirkwood; **106** Macdonald Orbis Archive; **107** National Trust Photographic Library/ J. Whitaker; **109, 111** By kind permission of Country Life; **112, 114, 115** National Trust for Scotland; **116** The British Architectural Library, RIBA, London; **117** Stephen Calloway; **118** National Trust Photographic Library/John Bethall; **121** Royal Commission on the Historical Monuments of England; **122** From 'The English Room' Derry Moore (Wiedenfield & Nicholson); **126/127** Ocean Designs, Edinburgh; **118** Reproduced by permission of Kettle's Yard, Cambridge; **130, 131, 132** By kind permission of Country Life; **134, 135** Macdonald Orbis Archive; **139, 140, 141** Petts Wood Residents Association/ Philip de Bay; **142** K. Stonor/Edward Piper; **144** Vogue (UK); **145** From 'Homes Sweet Homes' Osbert Lancaster, John Murray (Publishers) Ltd; **146** Angus McBean; **148** Millar & Harris; **149 left** By kind permission of Country Life; **149 right** Port Lympne Zoo Park, Mansions & Gardens, Hythe, Kent; **153, 158** By courtesy of the Board of Trustees of the Victoria & Albert Museum; **159, 161, 163** Stephen Calloway; **164** Graham Miller/ Homes & Gardens/World Press Network Ltd 1989; **166, 167** The British Architectural Library, RIBA, London; **168** World of Interiors/James Mortimer; **170, 171** House & Garden, Conde Nast Publications Ltd; **172** House & Garden/Arthur Sanderson & Sons Ltd; **177** Knoll International; **178** David Hicks International; **180** Michael Inchbald; **182** The Robert Harding Picture Library; **184** Arthur Sanderson & Sons Ltd; **186** EWA/ Tim Street-Porter; **188** Stephen Calloway; **189** EWA/Tim Street-Porter; **190** Anthony Redmile; **203** Christopher Wray.

Commissioned photography by Andreas von Einsiedel, Jerry Tubby and Philip de Bay.
Additional artwork by Bobbie Colgate-Stone.

The publishers have made every effort to trace the copyright holders of all transparencies and prints used in this publication. We apologise for any unintentional omissions and would be pleased to insert the appropriate acknowledgements in any subsequent editions.

The publishers have made every effort to ensure that all information listed in the directory relating to suppliers and their products is correct at the time of going to press. We apologise for any unintentional omissions or errors and would be pleased to include and/or correct them in any subsequent editions.